# Dulce

## Desserts from Santa Fe Kitchens

### THE MUSEUM OF
### NEW MEXICO FOUNDATION

GIBBS SMITH

TO ENRICH AND INSPIRE HUMANKIND

Salt Lake City | Charleston | Santa Fe | Santa Barbara

First Edition
12 11 10 09 08     5 4 3 2 1

Published by
Gibbs Smith
P.O. Box 667
Layton, Utah 84041

1-800.835.4993 orders
www.gibbs-smith.com

Designed and produced by Linda Herman, Glyph Publishing Arts
Printed and bound in China
Gibbs Smith books are printed on either recycled, 100% post consumer waste, or FSC certified papers.

Library of Congress Cataloging-in-Publication Data

Dulce : desserts from Santa Fe kitchens / the Museum of New Mexico
Foundation.—1st ed.
     p. cm.
  Includes index.
  ISBN-13: 978-1-4236-0489-1
  ISBN-10: 1-4236-0489-X
  1.  Desserts—New Mexico—Santa Fe. 2.  Cookery, American—Southwestern
style.  I. Museum of New Mexico Foundation.
  TX773.D8145 2008
  641.8'6—dc22
                       2008011147

Endsheets inspired by anonymous artist, *Window Flowers for New Year's*, c. 1950. Shanxi Province, China. Cut paper, 8-1/2 x 4-1/2 inches. Alexander Girard Foundation Collection, Museum of International Folk Art, Santa Fe, New Mexico. Photograph by Michel Monteaux. A.1981.39.941.

William Lumpkins, *Spanish Village*, 1934. Watercolor and pencil on board with plaster, 48 x 72-1/2 inches. On long term loan to the New Mexico Museum of Art from the U.S. General Services Administration, Public Works of Art Project.

Stafford Potteries. *Figure of Dick Turpin*, c.1865. Staffordshire, England. Glazed earthenware, 19-1/2 in. high. Alexander Girard Foundation Collection. Museum of International Folk Art. Photograph by Michael Monteaux. A.1981.42.239.

# Contents

# Introduction

FOR CENTURIES, Santa Fe has charmed visitors and captured the imagination and spirit of its residents. A central ingredient of Santa Fe's charm has been the kitchens of the city and the surrounding area. Whether in the home or in restaurants, Santa Fe kitchens reflect the diversity of its residents and visitors. Blending the diverse cultures of New Mexico—Native American, Hispanic, Anglo, and others—Santa Fe kitchens daily create a unique and compelling cuisine that is both local and international in its tastes and appeal.

The Museum of New Mexico Foundation, a private nonprofit organization dedicated to the four museums and six historical state monuments that comprise the Museum of New Mexico, sought recipes from its membership, local chefs, artists, and dignitaries to create this cookbook, *Dulce: Desserts from Santa Fe Kitchens*, which you now hold. Out of more than 1,000 recipes submitted for consideration, the experts on the Museum of New Mexico Foundation's Cookbook Committee selected more than 200 for this book. The recipes in the cookbook reflect the balance of Santa Fe's cultures and lifestyle: simple and complex, artistic and basic, fun yet challenging, and, of course, spicy yet with unbelievable sweetness.

No book produced by the Museum of New Mexico Foundation on Santa Fe kitchens would be complete without a discussion of the wonderful cultural institutions the Foundation supports. Throughout the book, specific artwork from the museums of New Mexico is shown, which displays the depth and quality of the art that can be seen at these museums. Below is a brief description of the museums and the Foundation. We urge you to support the museums by purchasing this cookbook, but also by visiting them often when in Santa Fe.

## The Museum of New Mexico Foundation

The Foundation envisions a Museum of New Mexico that will have ever-increasing financial resources and support, stronger private-public partnerships, and broader community participation. Our philanthropy, stewardship, and leadership will help strengthen the Museum of New Mexico's ability to create engaging cultural experiences for all New Mexico residents and visitors.

We promote excellence at the Museum of New Mexico through effective fundraising, innovative entrepreneurial ventures, community collaboration, and essential support services. For more information about The Museum of New Mexico Foundation, visit www.museumfoundation.org.

## The Palace of the Governors

The Palace of the Governors, built in 1609 and 1610, is the state history museum for New Mexico and is housed in the oldest continuously occupied public building in the United States. Exhibits, collections, and archives at the Palace of the Governors reflect the Spanish colonial (1540–1821), Mexican (1821–1846), U.S. territorial (1846–1912) and statehood (1912–present) periods of New Mexico history. The collection consists of more than 15,000 catalogued objects, many of which were donated to the Museum of New Mexico in the 1970s by the Historical Society of New Mexico. For more information about the Palace of the Governors, visit their Web site at www.palaceofthegovernors.org.

## The New Mexico Museum of Art, Santa Fe

The New Mexico Museum of Art was founded in 1917 as the Art Gallery of the Museum of New Mexico. Housed in a spectacular Pueblo Revival building designed by I. H. and William M. Rapp, it was based on their New Mexico building at the Panama-California Exposition (1915). The museum's architecture inaugurated what has come to be known as "Santa Fe Style."

The building combines aspects of several Southwestern regional styles, including elements of the facades of the Spanish mission churches of Acoma, Laguna, and San Felipe pueblos.

For more than eighty-five years the Museum has collected and exhibited work by artists from New Mexico. When the Museum of Art opened its doors in 1917, it was also a collecting institution. The earliest donations of works to the Museum of Art include paintings by artists who were active in the early days of the Taos and Santa Fe art communities.

Today, the Museum of Art's holdings number more than 23,000 objects, focusing on the areas of photography and works on paper; paintings, sculpture, and furniture from the twentieth century; and contemporary art. There is particular emphasis on work produced in or related to New Mexico. For more information about the Museum of Art, visit their Web site at www.mfasantafe.org.

## Museum of International Folk Art

The Museum of International Folk Art opened to the public in 1953 and has gained national and international recognition as the home to the world's largest collection of folk art. The collection of more than 130,000 artifacts forms the basis for exhibitions in four distinct wings: Girard, Hispanic Heritage, Bartlett, and Neutrogena.

The Girard Wing's popular permanent exhibition, Multiple Visions: A Common Bond, showcases folk art, popular art, toys, and textiles from more than one hundred nations. The late Alexander Girard, who contributed his immense collection to the museum, designed this unorthodox and delightful exhibition, which opened in 1982.

The Hispanic Heritage Wing introduces the culture of northern New Mexico, and its permanent exhibition, Family y Fe/Family and Faith, focuses on two of the strongest currents that continue to shape regional life today. Spanning four centuries from the Spanish colonial period to the twentieth century, the exhibition presents hide paintings, tinwork, furniture, jewelry, straw appliqué, horse gear, weavings, and santos, three-dimensional bultos and painted retablos. A changing gallery features artists representing living artistic traditions from vibrant and varied Hispano/Latino cultures.

The Bartlett Wing, named in honor of museum founder Florence Dibell Bartlett, has two galleries that offer rotating exhibitions based on the museum collections and on field studies of specific cultures or art forms. Exhibitions in this wing have ranged from Turkish, Tibetan, and Swedish traditions to New Deal–era art in New Mexico, recycled objects, and mayólica. Recent exhibitions include 100 Aspects of the Moon: Japanese Woodblockprints by Yoshitoshi; Dressing Up: Children's Clothes from Around the World; and Vernacular Visionaries: International Outsider Art in Context.

The Neutrogena Wing encompasses the Cotsen Gallery and Lloyd's Treasure Chest. The gallery provides an ideal setting for exhibitions featuring textiles from the museum's renowned collection, which now includes the Neutrogena Collection, a gift to the museum from Lloyd Cotsen and the Neutrogena Corporation in 1995. This international collection contains exquisite textiles and garments as well as objects. The Treasure Chest attracts all ages and invites visitors to explore what goes on behind the scenes in a museum. The Neutrogena Wing opened in 1998, expanding upon an ongoing public-private partnership that has characterized the museum's profile since its inception. For more information on the Museum of International Folk Art, visit www.moifa.org.

## The Museum of Indian Arts and Culture

At the Museum of Indian Arts and Culture (MIAC), one can encounter native cultures of the Southwest from ancestral to contemporary times. You can see art, material culture, and archaeology from a collection of more than 100,000 pieces, which includes some of the area's most treasured jewelry, baskets, pottery, and weaving. More than 65,000 visitors come to the Museum of Indian Arts and Culture each year, of which 30 percent hail from New Mexico, 50 percent from other states, and 20 percent from foreign countries. It is the mission of the Museum of Indian Arts and Culture to provide cross-cultural education to the many visitors to Santa Fe who take part in our programs and to New Mexican residents throughout the state. It is especially important that MIAC serve the Indian communities in the state and throughout the Southwest whose contemporary and ancestral cultures are represented in the museum's collections. For more information on the Museum of Indian Arts and Culture, visit www.miaclab.org.

# Chocolate Olé

## Flourless Chocolate Cake

### CAKE

12 ounces bittersweet or semisweet chocolate, chopped

3/4 cup unsalted butter, cut in pieces

6 large eggs, separated

12 tablespoons sugar, divided

2 teaspoons vanilla extract

### GANACHE

1/2 cup whipping cream

1/2 cup dark corn syrup

4 ounces bittersweet or semisweet chocolate, finely chopped

SERVES 8

*For the cake:* Preheat oven to 350 degrees F. Butter a 9-inch springform pan. Line bottom of pan with parchment or waxed paper, and butter paper. Wrap outside of pan with aluminum foil. Stir chocolate and butter in a heavy medium saucepan over low heat until melted and smooth. Remove from heat and cool to lukewarm, stirring often.

Using an electric mixer, beat egg yolks and 6 tablespoons sugar in a large bowl until mixture is very thick and pale, about 3 minutes. Fold lukewarm chocolate mixture into yolk mixture; then fold in vanilla extract. Using clean, dry beaters, beat egg whites in another large bowl until soft peaks form. Gradually add the remaining sugar, beating until medium-firm peaks form. Fold egg whites into the chocolate mixture in three additions. Pour batter into prepared pan.

Bake cake until top is puffed and cracked and tester inserted into center comes out with some moist crumbs attached, about 50 minutes. Cool cake in pan on a rack. Cake will fall.

Gently press down crusty top to make an evenly thick cake. Using a small knife, cut around the pan sides to loosen cake. Remove pan sides. Place a 9-inch diameter tart pan bottom, or a large enough plate, on top of the cake. Invert cake onto it. Peel off parchment paper.

*For the ganache:* Bring cream and corn syrup to a simmer in a medium saucepan. Remove from heat. Add chocolate and whisk until melted and smooth. Place cake on a rack set over a baking sheet. Spread 1/2 cup ganache smoothly over the top and sides of the cake. Freeze until almost set, about 3 minutes. Pour remaining ganache over cake; smooth sides and top. Place cake on a serving platter. Chill until ganache is firm, about 1 hour.

*Garnishes:* Sprinkle chocolate shavings over the top. Make chocolate leaves out of ganache and arrange decoratively. Pipe whipped cream rosettes around the edge and top each with a strawberry or raspberry.

*Can be made 1 day ahead, covered with cake dome, and stored at room temperature.*

Gene Kloss (1903-96), *The Sanctuary, Chimayo,* 1936. Etching and aquatint, 24 x 20 inches. On long-term loan from the U.S. General Services Administration, Works Progress Administration, Federal Arts project, 1936. New Mexico Museum of Art.

# Quail Run Chocolate Ganache with Raspberry Coulis

### CRUST
2 cups pecans

1/4 cup butter, melted

1 cup sugar

### GANACHE
8 ounces Belgian white chocolate

4 cups heavy cream, divided

8 ounces Belgian dark chocolate

### COULIS
1 cup sugar

1 package frozen raspberries

1 teaspoon vanilla extract

*For the crust:* Chop pecans in a food processor until fine. Transfer to a bowl and add butter and sugar. Mix well. Press mixture into a 10-inch tart pan with a removable bottom. Bake at 350 degrees F for 20 minutes, or until golden brown. Refrigerate crust until completely cooled.

*For the ganache:* Melt white chocolate in a double boiler. Whisk in 2 cups of cream and set aside. Repeat process with dark chocolate. Place bowl of white chocolate in an ice bath and whisk vigorously until stiff and the consistency of mousse. Repeat with dark chocolate.

Scoop both chocolates into the cooled crust, alternating between white and dark chocolates. With a toothpick, make swirls and peaks out of top of chocolate. Cool for at least 1 hour.

*For the coulis:* Bring all ingredients to a boil. Purée in a blender, then strain. Cool for at least 2 hours in the refrigerator.

To serve, dribble coulis over individual servings.

—*Paul Hunsicker, Executive Chef, Quail Run*

# 1800s Baked Fudge

SERVES 12 TO 15

4 eggs, well beaten

2 cups sugar

1/2 cup flour

1/2 cup dark cocoa powder

1 cup pecans, chopped

1 teaspoon vanilla extract

1/2 teaspoon salt

1 cup butter, melted

1 pint whipping cream, sweetened to taste, whipped, and chilled

Beat eggs and add sugar, flour, cocoa powder, pecans, vanilla, and salt; mix well. Stir in melted butter. Pour into a 9 x 12-inch glass dish. Place dish in a large roasting pan. Fill roasting pan with boiling water until water reaches halfway up the sides of the glass baking dish. Bake at 300 degrees F for 1 hour. (The fudge should have a light crust on top with an almost liquid center.) Top with whipped cream.

*Unbelievably rich and decadent!*

Unidentified photographer, *Pueblo Woman Grinding Corn*, c. 1910–1920. Collection of the Palace of the Governors Photo Archives.

# Chocolate Hearts with Coffee Anglaise

## HEARTS

2 ounces semisweet chocolate

1-1/4 cups milk

1/2 cup sifted cocoa

1/4 cup butter

2/3 cup sugar

3 egg yolks

1 envelope unflavored gelatin

1/4 cup water

1-1/4 cups heavy cream

## ANGLAISE

1 cup milk

3 tablespoons sugar, divided

2 teaspoons instant coffee powder

3 egg yolks

SERVES 8

*For the hearts:* Melt the chocolate in the top of a double boiler set over simmering water. Allow to cool. Place milk, cocoa, butter, and sugar in a saucepan and bring to a boil.

In a bowl, beat the egg yolks until creamy and mix with the melted chocolate. Strain into the hot milk mixture and whisk well.

In a small bowl, soften the gelatin in the water and add to the chocolate custard mixture. Stir well to make sure the gelatin is completely dissolved; cool.

In a large bowl, whip the cream to soft peaks. Fold in the cooled chocolate mixture with a metal spoon. Pour into eight small heart-shaped molds and refrigerate overnight.

*For the anglaise:* Put the milk in a heavy-bottomed saucepan with 2 tablespoons sugar and instant coffee powder. Bring to a boil; turn off the heat and stir until the coffee has dissolved.

In a large bowl, beat the egg yolks with the remaining sugar until white and fluffy. Pour into the hot coffee–milk, stirring well. Return the mixture to the saucepan, place over low heat and cook, stirring all the time, until the custard coats the back of the spoon. Remove from the stove and strain into a bowl. Cover the surface of the coffee anglaise with plastic wrap; cool and refrigerate. This can be made the day before.

To serve, unmold each chocolate heart onto a chilled dessert plate. Spoon a little coffee anglaise on each side of the heart.

# Bittersweet Chocolate Marquise
## with Cherry Sauce

10 ounces bittersweet or semi-sweet chocolate, chopped

3/4 cup unsalted butter, at room temperature, divided

1/2 cup sugar, divided

2 tablespoons unsweetened cocoa, sifted

4 large egg yolks

1/4 cup water

1 tablespoon vanilla extract

1 cup whipping cream, chilled

SAUCE

2 cups fresh cherries, pitted and halved

1/2 cup water

1/3 cup sugar

2 teaspoons Kirsch

1 tablespoon fresh lemon juice

2-1/2 teaspoons cornstarch

1/2 teaspoon grated lemon zest

SERVES 10 TO 12

*For the marquise:* Butter an 8-1/2 x 5-1/2 x 3-inch glass loaf dish. Line dish smoothly with foil. Stir chocolate in the top of a double boiler over barely simmering water until smooth. Turn off heat. Using an electric mixer, beat 1/2 cup butter in a large bowl until fluffy. Beat in 1/4 cup sugar, and then cocoa powder.

Whisk yolks, water, vanilla, remaining butter, and remaining sugar in a metal bowl. Set over saucepan of simmering water (do not let bowl touch water). Whisk constantly until candy thermometer registers 160 degrees F, about 6 minutes. Remove from over water. Using an electric mixer, beat the yolk mixture until thick and cool, about 5 minutes. Beat into cocoa mixture. Whip the cream in another bowl until soft peaks form. Fold into chocolate mixture; spread in prepared dish. Cover and chill until firm, at least 4 hours. Can be made 4 days ahead. Keep chilled.

*For the sauce:* Mix all ingredients in a medium saucepan over medium heat, until sauce boils and thickens, about 5 minutes; cool slightly. Can be made 2 days ahead. Cover and refrigerate. Rewarm before serving.

To serve, turn marquise out onto a platter; peel off foil. Cut into 3/4-inch-thick slices. Place 1 slice on each plate. Spoon warm cherry sauce over and serve immediately.

*This dessert is a dense and rich chocolate mousse–like cake in a mold.*

# Chocolate-Espresso Lava Cake
# with Espresso Whipped Cream

**CAKE**

1 cup flour

3/4 cup unsweetened cocoa powder

5 teaspoons instant espresso powder (or instant coffee powder)

1-1/2 teaspoons baking powder

1 cup butter, melted

1 cup sugar

1 cup firmly packed brown sugar

4 large eggs

1-1/2 teaspoons vanilla extract

1/4 teaspoon almond extract

12 tablespoons semisweet chocolate chips (about 4-1/2 ounces)

**CREAM**

1 cup chilled whipping cream

3 tablespoons confectioners' sugar

1 teaspoon instant espresso powder (or instant coffee powder)

SERVES 6

*For the cake:* Sift flour, cocoa powder, espresso powder, and baking powder into a medium bowl. Place butter in a large bowl; add sugars and whisk until well blended. Whisk in eggs, 1 at a time, and then the vanilla and almond extracts.

Whisk in dry ingredients. Divide batter among six 8-ounce ramekins or soufflé dishes. Top each with 2 tablespoons chocolate chips. Gently press chips into batter. Cover and refrigerate at least 1 hour and up to 1 day.

*For the cream:* Combine whipping cream, confectioners' sugar, and espresso powder in a medium bowl; whisk until peaks form. Chill up to 1 hour.

Position rack in center of the oven and preheat to 350 degrees F. Let ramekins with batter stand at room temperature for 5 minutes. Bake uncovered until cakes are puffed and crusty and a tester inserted into center comes out with thick batter attached, about 30 minutes. Cool for 5 minutes. Top with espresso whipped cream and serve.

Charles Craig (1846–1931), *Interior Courtyard of Pueblo, Santa Clara, New Mexico,* c. 1883. Oil on canvas, 21 1/2 x 39 1/2 in. Collection of New Mexico Museum of Art. Gift of Mr. and Mrs. John A. Hill in memory of Maurice N. Mikesell, 1975. Photograph by Blair Clark.

# Bittersweet Chocolate and Cranberry Terrine

SERVES 16

## CRANBERRIES

1 cup sugar

1 cup water

1-1/2 cups cranberries

## FILLING

1 cup whipping cream

4 egg yolks

3/4 cup sugar

12 ounces bittersweet chocolate

1 teaspoon vanilla extract

1 teaspoon orange zest

1 cup unsalted butter, at room
temperature

1 cup unsweetened cocoa powder

3/4 cup whipping cream, chilled

## CRANBERRY COULIS

4 cups cranberries

1-1/2 cups orange juice

1 cup sugar

2 tablespoons orange zest

2 tablespoons Grand Marnier or
Triple Sec

## TOPPING

1 cup whipped cream, sweetened
to taste

8 (1/3 x 2-inch) orange peel strips

1 cup toasted almonds, chopped

*For the cranberries:* Place wire rack atop a baking sheet. Stir sugar and water in a heavy medium saucepan over medium heat until sugar dissolves. Boil without stirring until syrup registers 234 degrees F on a candy thermometer. Stir in cranberries until they are coated with syrup and begin to pop, about 4 minutes. Using slotted spoon, transfer cranberries to the prepared rack; cover and refrigerate. Can be prepared 1 day ahead.

*For the filling:* Bring 1 cup cream to a simmer in a heavy medium saucepan. Whisk yolks and sugar in a small bowl to blend. Gradually whisk hot cream into yolk mixture. Return mixture to saucepan and stir over medium heat until mixture thickens and leaves a path on the back of a spoon when finger is drawn across, about 6 minutes. Do not boil. Remove from heat and add chocolate. Stir until chocolate melts and mixture is smooth. Add vanilla and orange zest. Cool custard to room temperature.

Line an 8-cup rectangular terrine or bread pan with aluminum foil. Using an electric mixer, beat butter and cocoa powder in a large bowl until light and fluffy. Gradually beat in custard. Whip 3/4 cup chilled cream in a large bowl to soft peaks. Fold into chocolate mixture. Spoon filling into prepared pan. Cover with plastic and refrigerate overnight. Can be prepared 4 days ahead.

*For the coulis:* Combine cranberries, orange juice, sugar, and orange zest in a heavy large saucepan. Simmer over medium heat until cranberries lose their shape and mixture thickens slightly, stirring occasionally, about 12 minutes. Transfer mixture to a processor and blend until smooth. Stir in liqueur. Can be prepared 4 days ahead. Makes 4 cups.

To serve, unmold terrine onto a platter; remove foil. Smooth top and sides with a spatula, if necessary. Spoon whipped cream into pastry bag fitted with a medium star tip. Pipe 16 rosettes down the center of the terrine. Top rosettes alternately with chilled reserved cranberries and orange peel strips. Cut terrine into thin slices and serve with the coulis and sprinkle with toasted almonds.

# Le Montmorency

## CAKE

8 ounces bittersweet or semi-sweet chocolate

1 tablespoon instant coffee powder

1/4 cup Kirsch

4 eggs, separated

3/4 cup unsalted butter

1/3 cup flour

1/3 cup sugar

## FILLING

1 pound fresh, pitted cherries (or canned bing cherries)

1/3 cup sugar

2 tablespoons Kirsch

## TOPPING

6 ounces bittersweet or semi-sweet chocolate

3 tablespoons water

2 tablespoons Kirsch

SERVES 10 TO 12

*For the cake:* Preheat oven to 375 degrees F. Grease a 9-inch springform pan and line with parchment paper. Melt chocolate, coffee powder, and Kirsch in a double boiler. Remove from heat and stir in egg yolks. Return to heat to thicken slightly. Remove from heat. Whisk in butter a little at a time; stir in flour.

In a separate bowl, beat egg whites until they create soft peaks; add sugar. Beat until stiff and shiny. Fold whites into chocolate mixture. Pour into a springform pan and bake 20 to 25 minutes, until puffed and a tester comes out slightly creamy from the center; cool. Cake will sink and crack.

*For the filling:* Poach cherries with sugar and Kirsch about 30 to 40 minutes to make a compote; cool and then chop roughly. Invert cake onto a plate and remove about a 5-inch circle from the center, leaving 1/2 inch at the bottom. Mix scooped-out cake with filling. Add mixture to the cake center. Press with a spatula to smooth top.

*For the topping:* Melt the chocolate in double boiler. Add water and Kirsch and heat through. Cool slightly and spread over cake.

—*Donna Nordin, Executive Chef, Terra Cotta Restaurant*

# Chocolate Fudge Pie

1 cup sugar

1/2 cup butter, melted

2 eggs

1/2 cup flour

Dash of salt

5 tablespoons cocoa powder

1 teaspoon vanilla

1/2 cup chopped pecans

SERVES 8

Preheat oven to 300 degrees F. In a large bowl, mix sugar and butter; beat until creamy. Add eggs, flour, salt, cocoa, and vanilla; beat well and stir in pecans.

Bake in a greased 8-inch pie pan until a tester comes out clean, about 30 minutes.

Serve with whipped cream or ice cream.

# Peppermint Brownies

2 ounces unsweetened chocolate

1/2 cup butter

2 eggs

1 cup sugar

1/4 teaspoon peppermint extract

1/2 cup flour

Pinch of salt

1/2 cup pecan pieces

ICING

1-1/2 cups confectioners' sugar

3 tablespoons butter, at room temperature

1 or 2 tablespoons evaporated milk

1/2 teaspoon peppermint extract

Drop of green food coloring

SERVES 15 TO 18

Preheat oven to 350 degrees F. Melt chocolate and butter in a small pan. In a large bowl, beat eggs with sugar, and then add chocolate mixture; stir well. Add remaining ingredients and stir to mix. Bake in a buttered 11 x 7-inch baking pan for 20 to 25 minutes. Cool.

*For the icing:* Combine all ingredients and blend until smooth and spreadable.

Ice brownies and keep refrigerated until ready to serve.

# Fudgy Adobe Brownies

8 ounces Scharffen Berger 70% bittersweet chocolate, chopped

6 tablespoons unsalted butter

1/4 teaspoon salt

1/2 teaspoon vanilla

1 scant cup sugar

2 large eggs

1/4 cup flour, sifted

1/2 to 1 cup walnut halves or pieces

SERVES 12 TO 16

Place rack in lower third of the oven and preheat to 325 degrees F. Butter or line an 8-inch square cake pan with parchment paper and set aside.

Heat the chocolate and butter in the top of a 3-quart double boiler or water bath. Stir occasionally until melted. If necessary, whisk to smooth. Remove from heat, stir in the salt, vanilla, and sugar. Add the eggs one at a time, stirring after each addition until incorporated.

Add the flour and stir briskly for about 1 minute, or until the mixture is smooth and shiny and comes away from the side of the pot. Stir in the nuts. Turn the mixture into the prepared cake pan and smooth the top. Bake for 35 to 40 minutes, or until a tester inserted into the center comes out moist but free of batter.

Remove from the oven. Cool on a rack. Cut into 2-inch squares. Serve warm or at room temperature.

Chicago Transparency Co., *Indian detour busses at La Fonda Hotel, Santa Fe*, c. 1910–1920. Collection of the Palace of Governors Photo Archives.

# Harry's Roadhouse Chocolate Cream Pie

1 pie shell

FILLING

2-1/2 cups milk

2/3 cup sugar

2 eggs

2 egg yolks

1/2 cup heavy cream

1/4 cup cornstarch, sifted

3 tablespoons cocoa

Pinch of salt

7 ounces bittersweet chocolate, finely chopped

3 tablespoons unsalted butter

1 teaspoon vanilla

TOPPING

1-1/2 cups heavy cream

3/4 cup confectioners' sugar

Chocolate curls for garnish

SERVES 6 TO 8

Prebake pie shell; set aside.

*For the filling:* Scald milk and sugar in a saucepan. Meanwhile, whisk together the eggs, egg yolks, cream, cornstarch, cocoa, and salt in a large bowl. Pour the scalded milk into the bowl and whisk until smooth. Pour back into the saucepan and bring to a boil, whisking the whole time.

Remove from heat and whisk in the chocolate, butter, and vanilla. Whisk until smooth and pour in the prepared pie shell. Place plastic wrap directly on top of the filling to keep a film from forming. Chill until cold, about 3 hours.

*For the topping:* Whip cream with sugar until stiff peaks have formed.

Serve chilled with the whipped cream and chocolate curls.

—*Harry's Roadhouse, Santa Fe*

# Chocolate Sorbet

3-1/4 cups plus 1 tablespoon water

1 cup sugar

3/4 cup plus 1 tablespoon unsweetened cocoa powder

9-3/4 ounces Scharffen Berger 70% bittersweet chocolate

In a medium saucepan, combine the 2-1/4 cups water and sugar. Bring to a boil over high heat, stirring occasionally. Gradually add cocoa, whisking until smooth. Reduce heat to low and cook mixture at a gentle simmer for 30 minutes, or until syrupy.

Place chocolate and half the cocoa syrup in a large bowl, whisking until chocolate is melted and mixture is smooth. Add remaining syrup and whisk well. Strain mixture through a fine sieve and let cool. Stir in 1 cup plus 1 tablespoon water.

Cover sorbet mixture and chill until very cold, at least 4 hours. Freeze in an ice cream maker according to manufacturer's directions.

# Chocolate Mousse Torte

8 ounces semisweet chocolate

1 tablespoon instant coffee powder

1/4 cup boiling water

8 eggs, separated

2/3 cup sugar

2-1/2 teaspoons vanilla, divided

1/8 teaspoon salt

1/4 cup fine breadcrumbs

1-1/2 cups whipping cream

1/4 cup sifted confectioners' sugar

SERVES 8

Preheat oven to 350 degrees F. Place chocolate in the top of a double boiler. Dissolve coffee in boiling water and then add to the chocolate; cover. Let stand over very low heat, stirring occasionally, until chocolate is melted and smooth.

In a separate bowl, beat egg yolks until thick. Gradually beat in sugar; beat until mixture is lemon colored. Slowly beat the chocolate into the egg mixture. Add 1 teaspoon vanilla.

In a separate bowl, beat egg whites and salt until stiff but not dry. Fold whites into chocolate mixture slowly until blended.

Butter and dust a 9-inch pie plate with breadcrumbs. Fill with mousse until just level with edge; refrigerate remainder. Bake for 25 minutes. Turn off oven; leave in 5 minutes longer. Cool 2 hours on a wire rack so that the mousse sinks in the middle to form a pie shell. Fill cooled pie shell with chilled uncooked mousse. Chill 2 hours.

To serve, beat whipping cream with remaining vanilla and confectioners' sugar. Spread over pie or use piping bag to make a lattice pattern.

# Cinnamon Ganache Tart

15 chocolate graham crackers (or 30 chocolate wafers)

2 tablespoons sugar

1/2 cup butter, melted, divided

1 (12-ounce) bag semisweet chocolate morsels

2/3 cup half-and-half

1/2 teaspoon ground cinnamon

1 pint raspberries (or blackberries)

SERVES 12

In a food processor, pulse crackers and sugar 2 minutes. Add 1/4 cup melted butter. Press mixture into a greased 9-inch tart pan with removable bottom; freeze 20 minutes.

In a bowl, combine chocolate morsels and remaining butter. In a saucepan, boil half-and-half and cinnamon. Pour over chocolate. Let sit 1 minute; stir. Spread in crust and top with berries right before serving.

# Bittersweet Chocolate Mousse

24 ounces bittersweet chocolate chips

1 egg yolk

1/3 cup amaretto liqueur

3-1/2 cups whipping cream

Melt chocolate chips in the top of a double boiler. Add egg yolk and amaretto and stir until smooth. Remove from heat.

Whip the cream until heavy peaks form. Add slightly cooled chocolate mixture and mix until well combined. Cover, place in refrigerator, and chill until ready to serve.

Garnish with fresh fruit and cookies.

# Spanish Chocolate Flan with Mint Sauce

FLAN

12 ounces bittersweet chocolate

1 cup sugar

1-1/2 cups butter

6 eggs

1 teaspoon cinnamon

2 tablespoons dark rum

SAUCE

2 tablespoons sugar

1/4 cup crème de menthe

1 cup crème fraîche

SERVES 8

*For the flan:* Preheat oven to 375 degrees F. In a saucepan, melt chocolate and cool slightly. In a separate bowl, cream together sugar and butter. Add the eggs and mix well. Stir in the chocolate, cinnamon, and rum.

Line a 9-inch round pan with removable rim with buttered parchment paper and cover the outside of the pan with aluminum foil so there is no chance of water from the water bath seeping into the flan. Pour in the chocolate mixture. Cover the top of the flan lightly with foil.

Place the flan mold into a large roasting pan and pour boiling water halfway up the sides of the flan mold. Bake for 30 minutes. Remove the foil top and bake for 10 minutes longer, or until the top of the flan is fairly firm. (However, the top should not poof up.) Remove flan from the oven and the water bath; cool to room temperature. When cool, refrigerate for several hours or overnight. Can be made ahead; it freezes well.

*For the sauce:* Dissolve the sugar in the crème de menthe and then stir into the crème fraîche. Allow flavors to mingle several hours or overnight. Can be made one day ahead.

To serve, unmold the flan and slice into 1-inch-thick wedges. Place slices on individual serving plates and pour a little sauce over or around each flan serving.

*This recipe originated in Figueres, Spain.*

Anonymous artist, *Straw Horse*, c. 1960. Nagano, Nagano Japan. Wrapped fiber, 7-3/8 inches high. Alexander Girard Foundation Collection. Museum of International Folk Art. Photograph by Michael Monteaux. A.1981.4.91Nagano.

# Chocolate Soufflé

1 tablespoon melted butter

4 ounces bittersweet chocolate

1/2 cup heavy cream

2 teaspoons extra-fine ground coffee

3 eggs, separated

2 tablespoons brandy

1/2 teaspoon vanilla

3 tablespoons extra-fine sugar

Confectioners' sugar

SERVES 2 TO 4

Preheat oven to 425 degrees F. Place oven rack in the lower third of the oven, providing enough room for the soufflé to rise.

Brush a 4-quart soufflé dish with melted butter and set aside. Coarsely chop the chocolate, and then process finely in a food processor. In a medium saucepan, combine the chocolate and cream, stirring until melted and smooth, about 5 minutes. Add the coffee. Remove from heat.

Add egg yolks, 1 at a time, whisking constantly until combined with the chocolate. Simmer about 4 minutes. Remove from the heat and whisk in the brandy and vanilla. Mixture can be refrigerated up to 4 hours, tightly covered.

Reheat mixture until just hot to the touch, stirring until smooth. Beat the egg whites until stiff. Continue beating while adding the extra-fine sugar. The mixture should become glossy in about 30 seconds. Fold a small amount of the egg whites into the chocolate until it is a thin consistency, and then fold in the rest of the whites, taking care not to overwork the batter. Gently fill the prepared soufflé dish and bake until puffed, about 15 to 20 minutes. Sprinkle decoratively with confectioners' sugar, using a cut template or a sieve or shaker. Serve immediately.

# Le Saveur Mocha Pots de Crème

3/4 cup whipping cream

6 ounces grated bittersweet or semisweet chocolate

2 teaspoons espresso

1 egg

2 tablespoons sugar

1 teaspoon vanilla

Pinch of salt

Whipped cream, coffee beans, and crystallized violets for garnish

SERVES 6 TO 8

Heat cream in a saucepan until bubbles form around the edges. Melt chocolate in a double boiler. Whisk cream and remaining ingredients into chocolate. Heat through and blend well, without whipping.

Pour into six to eight individual ramekins and chill until firm.

Garnish with a dollop of whipped cream and coffee bean or crystallized violet.

—Dee Rusanowski, owner, Le Saveur Restaurant

# Mexican Hot Chocolate Ice Cream

1 cup milk

5 to 6 ounces "chocolate para mesa" (e.g., 4 tablets Abuelita brand)

1/4 cup sugar

1 teaspoon vanilla

2 cups heavy cream, chilled

3 heaping tablespoons red chili powder

SERVES 8

Heat milk until it bubbles around the edges. Crack the chocolate pieces into bits with a kitchen hammer. Add chocolate and sugar to hot milk and whisk vigorously until chocolate is melted and sugar is dissolved; chill well.

Add vanilla and cream, whisking until totally mixed. Add chili powder and whisk again to mix. Freeze according to ice cream maker's instructions. Serve immediately.

*Can be kept in the freezer for a week. Don't worry about the amount of chili, you may want more. The combination of chocolate, dairy, and freezing diminishes the heat greatly. Serve with biscochitos or sugar cookies.*

# Bravo for Cookies!

## Supernatural Brownies

8 ounces bittersweet chocolate

1 cup unsalted butter

4 large eggs

1/2 teaspoon salt

1 cup firmly packed dark brown sugar

2 teaspoons vanilla

1 cup flour

1/2 cup chopped walnuts, pecans, almonds, or hazelnuts (optional)

MAKES 24 TO 30 BROWNIES

Preheat oven to 350 degrees F. Butter a 9 x 13-inch baking pan and line with buttered parchment paper.

In a double boiler, melt chocolate and butter and stir until smooth; cool slightly. Beat eggs with an electric mixer and then add salt, sugar, and vanilla, blending well. Add chocolate mixture. Add flour and mix until just combined. Mix in nuts, if using.

Pour into prepared pan. Bake for 45 to 50 minutes, until shiny and beginning to crack on top. Cool in pan on rack. Cut into squares.

## Mexican Chocolate Brownies

6 tablespoons unsalted butter, cut into pieces

3 ounces premium bittersweet chocolate, chopped

2 ounces premium unsweetened chocolate, chopped

1 cup sugar

1/2 cup whole blanched almonds, toasted until golden and cooled

2 large eggs

1/2 cup flour

1/2 teaspoon salt

1/2 teaspoon cinnamon

MAKES 16 BROWNIES

Preheat oven to 350 degrees F. In a heavy medium saucepan, melt butter and chocolate over low heat, stirring until smooth. Remove from heat and cool for 10 minutes. Process sugar and almonds in a food processor until finely ground. Stir almond mixture into chocolate mixture and add eggs, one at a time, beating well with a large wooden spoon until mixture is glossy and smooth. Stir in flour, salt, and cinnamon until just combined.

Spread batter in a 9-inch square baking pan that has been greased and dusted with flour. Bake 25 to 30 minutes, or until tester inserted in center comes out with moist crumbs attached. Cool brownies completely in pan on rack; cut into squares. Brownies can be stored in an airtight container for 5 days or frozen.

Anonymous artist, *Kantha Textile (detail)*, late nineteenth century. West Bengal, India. Embroidered cotton on cotton, 77-5/8 x 53-1/8 in. Alexander Girard Foundation Collection. Museum of International Folk Art. Photograph by Michael Monteaux. AGEx.001.

# Rum-Raisin Chocolate Brownies

1 cup raisins

1/4 cup dark rum

3/4 cup unsalted butter

4 ounces unsweetened chocolate

2 cups sugar

4 large eggs

3/4 cup flour

1 cup semisweet chocolate chips

MAKES 24 TO 30 BROWNIES

Preheat oven to 350 degrees F. Butter and flour a 9 x 13-inch metal baking pan. Soak raisins in rum until plump, about 30 minutes. In a heavy medium saucepan over medium heat, stir butter and unsweetened chocolate together until smooth. Transfer to a large bowl and cool slightly. Whisk in sugar and eggs, one at a time, beating until mixture is smooth. With a large spoon, mix in raisins with rum. Add in flour until just combined. Stir in chocolate chips. Pour batter into pan. Bake until tester inserted into center comes out with moist crumbs attached, about 25 minutes. Cool brownies in pan on a rack. Cut into squares.

# Butterscotch Brownies

1/2 cup unsalted butter

2 cups firmly packed light brown sugar

2 large eggs

1 cup sifted flour

2 teaspoons baking powder, sifted with flour

1 teaspoon salt, sifted with flour

1 teaspoon vanilla

1 cup pecans, coarsely chopped

MAKES 24 (2-INCH SQUARE) BROWNIES

Preheat oven to 350 degrees F. Melt butter in a medium saucepan over low heat. Add brown sugar and stir until well blended. Remove from heat and allow mixture to cool slightly. Transfer to the bowl of an electric mixer and beat in eggs. Mix in sifted dry ingredients until just combined. Add vanilla and nuts. Spread into a greased and floured 9 x 13-inch pan. Bake for 25 to 30 minutes, until golden and edges have pulled away slightly from sides of pan. Remove and let cool about 20 minutes. Cut while still warm and watch them disappear!

# Apricot Bars

1-1/3 cups dried apricots

1 cup unsalted butter, at room temperature

1/2 cup sugar

2-2/3 cups sifted flour, divided

4 large eggs, well beaten

2 cups firmly packed light brown sugar

1 teaspoon baking powder

1/2 teaspoon salt

1 teaspoon vanilla

1 cup chopped pecans

Confectioners' sugar, for dusting

MAKES 24 TO 30 BARS

Preheat oven to 375 degrees F. In a small saucepan, cover apricots with water and simmer for 10 minutes, or until soft. Drain, cool, and chop; set aside.

Mix butter, sugar, and 2 cups flour in a large bowl until crumbly. Press into two greased and floured 8 x 8-inch pans or one 9 x 13-inch baking pan. Bake for 25 minutes.

Place eggs into the large bowl of an electric mixer; gradually add brown sugar and beat until light and fluffy. Sift remaining flour, baking powder, and salt together. Add dry ingredients, vanilla, nuts, and apricots. Spread over baked layer in the pan. Bake 30 minutes. When cool, cut into bars and dust with confectioners' sugar.

# Date Bars

1 cup sugar

3 large eggs, beaten

1 teaspoon vanilla

1 cup flour

1 teaspoon baking powder

1/4 teaspoon salt

1/4 teaspoon ground cloves

1/2 teaspoon ground cinnamon

2 cups chopped dates

1 cup chopped nuts

2 tablespoons flax seeds, or more, to taste, optional

Confectioners' sugar, for dusting

MAKES 24 (2-INCH SQUARE) BARS

Preheat oven to 325 degrees F. Beat sugar and eggs together with an electric mixer until light and fluffy, about 3 minutes; add vanilla and set aside. Sift flour, baking powder, salt, and spices in another bowl. Stir in dates, nuts, and flax seed, if using. Add dry ingredients to sugar mixture and blend until well combined. Spread batter into a greased and floured 9 x 13-inch pan. Bake for 25 to 30 minutes. When cool, cut into bars and dust with confectioners' sugar.

# Sour Cream Apple Squares

CRUST

2 cups flour

2 cups firmly packed light brown sugar

1/2 cup butter, at room temperature

1 cup chopped walnuts

APPLE LAYER

1-1/2 teaspoons cinnamon

1 teaspoon baking soda

1/2 teaspoon salt

1 cup sour cream

1 teaspoon vanilla

1 large egg

2 cups (2 medium) Granny Smith apples, peeled and finely chopped

MAKES 16 TO 20 SQUARES

*For the crust:* Preheat oven to 350 degrees F. In a large mixer bowl, combine flour, brown sugar, and butter. Blend together at low speed until crumbly. Stir in nuts. Press 2-3/4 cups crumb mixture into an ungreased 9 x 13-inch baking pan.

*For the apple layer:* To remaining crumb mixture, add cinnamon, baking soda, salt, sour cream, vanilla, and egg, blending until well incorporated. Stir in apples. Spread batter evenly over base layer. Bake 25 to 35 minutes, or until a tester inserted in the center comes out clean. Cut into squares when cool.

*If desired, cut into larger squares and top with whipped cream.*

# Cheesecake Squares

MAKES 24 (2-INCH) SQUARES

**CRUST**

2/3 cup firmly packed light brown sugar

2/3 cup finely chopped walnuts or pecans

2 cups flour

1/2 cup unsalted butter, melted

**FILLING**

2 (8-ounce) packages cream cheese

1/2 cup sugar

3 large eggs

2 tablespoons fresh lemon juice

4 tablespoons heavy cream or milk

2 teaspoons vanilla

*For the crust:* Preheat oven to 350 degrees F. Mix all ingredients together until crumbly. Reserve 1 cup of the crust mixture for topping. Press remaining dough firmly into a 9 x 13-inch pan. Bake for 12 to 15 minutes.

*For the filling:* Place cream cheese and sugar in a large mixer bowl; beat at medium-high speed until smooth. Add eggs, one at a time, then lemon juice, cream, and vanilla and beat until well combined. Pour mixture into baked crust. Top with reserved crumb mixture and bake about 25 minutes. Cool and refrigerate. Cut into desired size when cooled.

*Cheesecake squares can be refrigerated for one week or frozen longer.*

# Butter Crunch Lemon-Cheese Bars

MAKES 16 (2-INCH SQUARE) BARS

**CRUST**

1/3 cup unsalted butter, at room temperature

1/4 cup firmly packed dark brown sugar

1/4 teaspoon salt

1/4 teaspoon ground nutmeg or mace

1 cup flour

**FILLING**

1 cup (1% low-fat) cottage cheese

1 cup sugar

2 tablespoons flour

1 tablespoon grated lemon zest

3-1/2 tablespoons fresh lemon juice

1/4 teaspoon baking powder

1 large egg

1 large egg white

*For the crust:* Preheat oven to 350 degrees F. Place first four ingredients in a large bowl and beat with a mixer at medium speed until well combined. Lightly spoon flour into a dry measuring cup and level. Add flour to butter mixture, and beat at low speed until well blended. Press crust into an 8-inch square baking pan coated with cooking spray. Bake for 20 minutes.

*For the filling:* Place cottage cheese in a food processor; process 2 minutes until smooth, scraping sides of bowl once. Add remaining ingredients and process until well blended. Pour filling over crust. Bake for 25 minutes, or until set (edges will get lightly browned). Cool; cover and chill for 8 hours. Serve chilled.

*Note: Fresh orange juice and grated orange zest may be substituted for lemon.*

Agnes Pelton (1881–1961), *Awakening*, 1943. Oil on canvas, 22 x 28 in. Collection of New Mexico Museum of Art. Photograph by Blair Clark.

# Lemon Bars

**CRUST**

1 cup unsalted butter

3/4 cup confectioners' sugar, plus more for dusting

2-1/4 cup unsifted flour

1/4 teaspoon salt

**FILLING**

4 eggs, lightly beaten

2 cups sugar

1/4 cup flour

1/4 cup fresh lemon juice

Finely grated zest of 1 lemon

MAKES 24 TO 30 BARS

*For the crust:* Preheat oven to 350 degrees F. Mix butter, confectioners' sugar, flour, and salt together until well combined. Press dough mixture firmly into a 9 x 13-inch pan. Bake for 15 to 20 minutes.

*For the filling:* While the crust is still hot, mix eggs, sugar, flour, lemon juice, and zest until well blended. Pour over crust. Bake for 25 minutes.

Dust with confectioners' sugar and cool before cutting.

# Coconut Lemon Sours

## CRUST
1 cup unsifted flour

2 tablespoons sugar

1/8 teaspoon salt

1/3 cup unsalted butter, at room
temperature

## COCONUT-LEMON LAYER
2 eggs, beaten

1 cup firmly packed brown sugar

1 tablespoon fresh lemon juice

1 teaspoon grated lemon zest

1/2 cup chopped nuts

1 cup flaked coconut, plus more
for garnish

## GLAZE
1 tablespoon or more fresh lemon
juice

1 teaspoon finely grated lemon zest

2/3 cup confectioners' sugar

MAKES 16 (2-INCH) SQUARES

*For the crust:* Preheat oven to 350 degrees F. Mix flour, sugar, and salt in a large bowl. Cut in butter. Press mixture into an ungreased 9-inch square pan. Bake for 15 minutes.

*For the coconut-lemon layer:* Combine all ingredients in a large bowl; mix well. Spread over crust and bake for 30 minutes.

*For the glaze:* Combine all ingredients. Spread glaze over top of sours and sprinkle with more coconut while still hot. When cool, cut into squares.

*Adobe buildings and horno, San Ildefonso Pueblo,* c.1910–1920. Collection of the Palace of the Governors Photo Archives.

# Sour Cream–Sugar Cookies

1/2 cup unsalted butter, at room temperature

1-1/4 cups sugar

1 large egg

1 teaspoon vanilla

1/2 teaspoon baking soda

1/2 cup sour cream

3 cups flour, divided

1-1/2 teaspoons baking powder

1/4 teaspoon salt

1/4 teaspoon ground nutmeg

Chocolate sprinkles and/or colored sugar for decoration

MAKES 48 COOKIES

Beat butter in the large bowl of an electric mixer until fluffy. Gradually add sugar and beat until light. Add egg and vanilla and beat again until fluffy. Stir baking soda into sour cream; mix well into butter mixture.

In a separate bowl, whisk together 2 cups flour, baking powder, salt, and nutmeg. With mixer on low speed, slowly add flour mixture into butter mixture. Add remaining flour, 1/4 cup at a time, until well combined. Form dough into two equal balls, flatten into disk shape, and wrap in plastic wrap. Store in refrigerator for 2 hours or overnight.

Preheat oven to 375 degrees F. Roll out cookie dough to 1/8 inch thickness on a lightly floured work surface. Cut into 3-inch circles and place 1/2 inch apart on greased baking sheets. Sprinkle lightly with sprinkles or sugar. Bake until golden brown, about 8 to 10 minutes. Transfer to wire racks to cool.

*For an evenly browned cookie, switch baking sheets from upper/lower oven rack positions halfway through baking.*

# Giant Chocolate Sugar Cookies

1-1/2 cups flour

1/2 cup premium unsweetened Dutch-process cocoa powder

1 teaspoon baking powder

1/2 teaspoon salt

1/2 cup unsalted butter, at room temperature

1-1/2 cups sugar

1/2 cup vegetable shortening (or 1/2 cup unsalted butter), melted and cooled*

1 large egg

1-1/2 teaspoons vanilla

MAKES 8 GIANT COOKIES

Preheat oven to 375 degrees F. Whisk together flour, cocoa powder, baking powder, and salt in a medium bowl; set aside.

Place butter and sugar into the bowl of an electric mixer fitted with paddle attachment. Mix on medium-high speed until pale and fluffy. Mix in shortening. Add egg and vanilla; mix until creamy. Reduce speed to low; gradually add flour mixture, and mix until just combined.

Using a 2-1/2-inch ice cream scoop, drop dough onto baking sheets lined with parchment paper or Silpat liner, spacing about 4 inches apart. Bake until edges are firm, 18 to 20 minutes. Let cool on sheets on wire racks. Cookies can be stored in an airtight container for up to 2 days.

*\*Use vegetable shortening for a crisp-edged cookie with a soft center or butter if a thinner, crunchy cookie is preferred.*

# Margaret's Old-World Icebox Cookies

3 cups sifted flour

1/2 teaspoon baking soda

1 teaspoon cinnamon

1 cup unsalted butter

3/4 cup sugar

3/4 cup firmly packed light brown sugar

1 large egg

1 teaspoon vanilla

1 teaspoon lemon juice

1/2 cup slivered almonds, warmed slightly to increase flavor

MAKES ABOUT 36 COOKIES

Preheat oven to 350 degrees F. Sift flour, baking soda, and cinnamon together; set aside.

Cream butter and sugars together with an electric mixer until light and fluffy. Add egg and beat for 1 minute. Add vanilla and lemon juice, blending well. Add the almonds, then add the dry ingredients and mix until incorporated. Shape dough into three rolls, two inches thick. Wrap in plastic wrap and chill until firm. Cut rolls into thin slices and bake on a greased baking sheet for 10 minutes. Cool on a rack.

*The rolls of dough freeze well; if frozen, thaw in the refrigerator and continue with recipe.*

# Butterscotch Refrigerator Cookies

3-1/2 cups flour

1/4 teaspoon salt

1 teaspoon baking soda

1/4 teaspoon cream of tartar

1 cup shortening

2 cups firmly packed brown sugar

1 large egg, well beaten

3 teaspoons evaporated milk

1 teaspoon vanilla

MAKES 48 TO 60 COOKIES

Combine flour, salt, baking soda, and cream of tartar; sift and set aside. Cream shortening in the bowl of an electric mixer; add sugar gradually, continuing to beat until light. Mix in egg and blend well. Add dry ingredients, thinning mixture with evaporated milk; then add vanilla and mix well. Shape dough into a roll. Wrap in plastic wrap and chill for 24 hours.

Preheat oven to 400 degrees F. Slice log into thin slices, about 1/4 inch thick, and place on lightly greased baking sheets. Bake 6 to 10 minutes.

*Chopped nuts may be added to cookie dough, if desired.*

Helen Cordero, *Nativity Scene*, c. 1964. Cochiti Pueblo, New Mexico. Slipped and painted earthenware. Alexander Girard Foundation Collection. Museum of International Folk Art. Photograph by Michael Monteaux. A.1979.53.101.

# Holiday Chocolate Chip Cookies

2 tablespoons finely grated orange zest

1 cup sugar

1/2 cup firmly packed light brown sugar

1 cup unsalted butter, at room temperature

2 extra-large eggs

1 teaspoon vanilla

2-1/4 cups flour

1 teaspoon baking soda

1 teaspoon salt

1-3/4 cups semisweet chocolate chips

1 cup chopped pecans

1 cup dried cranberries or red and green candied cherries, coarsely chopped

MAKES ABOUT 48 COOKIES

Preheat oven to 375 degrees F. Combine orange zest with sugars. Add sugar mixture to butter in the large bowl of electric mixer and beat until light and fluffy, about 3 minutes. Add eggs and vanilla. Sift flour, baking soda, and salt together. Add to creamed mixture and mix well. Stir in chocolate chips, nuts, and cranberries. Drop cookie dough by heaping teaspoons or tablespoons, about two inches apart, onto greased or Silpat-lined baking sheets. Bake 15 to 20 minutes, or until lightly browned. If using two sheets at a time, exchange sheets from upper/lower oven racks positions halfway through baking. Transfer to racks for cooling.

*If dried cranberries are hard rather than semisoft, soak them in warm water, about 20 minutes, to plump them up; this will yield a chewier and more flavorful cookie.*

# Orange-Pecan Chocolate Chip Cookies

2 cups flour

1 tablespoon baking powder

1/2 teaspoon salt

1/2 cup plus 2 tablespoons unsalted butter, at room temperature

1 cup firmly packed light brown sugar

1/2 cup sugar

1 tablespoon finely grated orange zest or 1/4 teaspoon orange extract

1 teaspoon vanilla

2 large eggs

1-1/2 cups semisweet chocolate chips

1-1/2 cups chopped pecans

MAKES 48 COOKIES

Preheat oven to 350 degrees F. Sift flour, baking powder, and salt together into a medium bowl; set aside. Cream butter, sugars, orange zest, and vanilla together with electric mixer until light and fluffy. Scrape bowl frequently. Add eggs, one at a time, and beat on medium speed after each addition until egg is incorporated. Add dry ingredients and mix on low speed until almost blended. Scrape bowl again. Add chocolate chips and nuts; mix well. Drop dough by tablespoons about 2 inches apart onto lightly greased baking sheets. Flatten them lightly. Bake until golden, about 15 minutes. Cool on sheets; cookies will crisp as they cool.

# Creamy Peanut Butter and Chocolate Chunk Cookies

1/2 cup unsalted butter, at room temperature

3/4 cup smooth peanut butter

1/2 cup sugar

1/2 cup firmly packed dark brown sugar

1 large egg

1/2 teaspoon vanilla

1 cup flour

3/4 teaspoon baking soda

1 (6-ounce) bar premium semisweet chocolate, broken into chunks

MAKES 14 LARGE COOKIES

Preheat oven to 350 degrees F. Cream butter, peanut butter, and sugars in the bowl of an electric mixer until light and fluffy, about 3 minutes. Add egg and vanilla, and mix well.

In a separate bowl, sift flour and baking soda together; add to the peanut butter mixture, beating just to combine. Fold in chocolate chunks.

Using a large spoon or a large ice-cream scoop, drop dough on a baking sheet lined with Silpat or parchment paper, pressing down slightly to flatten. Bake for 18 to 20 minutes, or until golden brown. Transfer to a wire rack and cool. Store cookies in an airtight container for up to 1 week.

# Chewy Chocolate Gingerbread Cookies

1-1/2 cups plus 1 tablespoon flour

1-1/4 teaspoons ground ginger

1 teaspoon ground cinnamon

1/4 teaspoon ground cloves

1/4 teaspoon nutmeg

1 tablespoon cocoa powder

1/2 cup unsalted butter

1 tablespoon fresh grated ginger

1/2 cup firmly packed dark brown sugar

1/4 cup molasses

1 teaspoon baking soda

1-1/2 teaspoons boiling water

7 ounces semisweet chocolate chips

1/4 cup sugar

MAKES ABOUT 24 COOKIES

In a medium bowl, sift together flour, ginger, cinnamon, cloves, nutmeg, and cocoa powder; set aside.

Place butter and ginger in the bowl of an electric mixer; beat until light, about 4 minutes. Add brown sugar and beat until combined. Add molasses, blending well.

Meanwhile, dissolve baking soda in boiling water. Beat half of the flour mixture into the butter mixture. Add the dissolved baking soda and then the remaining flour mixture. Stir in chocolate chips. Turn out onto plastic wrap and pat dough 1 inch thick. Wrap and refrigerate 2 hours.

Preheat oven to 325 degrees F. Roll dough into balls and refrigerate 20 minutes. Before baking, roll balls in sugar and place on lightly greased baking sheets. Bake for approximately 13 to 15 minutes.

# Di Di's Oatmeal and Chocolate Chip Cookies

1 cup unsalted butter

1-1/2 cups firmly packed dark brown sugar

2 large eggs

2 teaspoons vanilla

1 teaspoon salt

1 teaspoon baking soda

1-1/3 cups sifted flour

2 cups regular oatmeal

1 cup chopped walnuts or pecans

12 ounces chocolate chips

MAKES 36 TO 48 COOKIES

Preheat oven to 350 degrees F. Cream butter and sugar with an electric mixer until fluffy; add eggs and beat until combined. Add vanilla, salt, baking soda, flour, and oatmeal and mix thoroughly. Mix in nuts and chocolate chips. Drop dough by teaspoons onto greased baking sheet. Bake for 14 to 16 minutes; cool. Store the cookies in a covered container.

# Death by Chocolate Cookies

16 ounces semisweet chocolate chips, divided

3/4 cup firmly packed light brown sugar

1/4 cup unsalted butter

2 large eggs, beaten

1 teaspoon vanilla

1/2 cup flour

1/4 teaspoon baking powder

2 cups chopped pecans

MAKES ABOUT 18 COOKIES

Preheat oven to 350 degrees F. Melt 8 ounces (1 cup) chocolate chips over low heat and stir until smooth. Transfer melted chocolate to the large bowl of an electric mixer; add brown sugar, butter, eggs, and vanilla, blending well. With mixer on low speed, blend in the flour and baking powder. Stir in remaining chocolate chips and pecans. Using a 1/4-cup measuring cup, drop dough onto an ungreased baking sheet. Bake 12 minutes, or until cookies are puffed and feel set to the touch. Cool on pan 1 minute. Transfer to a wire rack and cool completely.

George Bellows (1882–1925), *Chimayo*, 1917. Oil on canvas, 30 x 40 in. Collection of New Mexico Museum of Art. Gift of the Museum of New Mexico Foundation, purchased from the Southwest Fine Arts Biennial, 1974. Photograph by Blair Clark.

# Toffee Cookies

1-1/2 cups unsalted butter

1-1/2 cups firmly packed dark brown sugar

2 egg yolks

3 cups sifted flour

1/2 teaspoon salt

2 teaspoons vanilla

12 ounces semisweet chocolate chips

1/2 cup chopped almonds, lightly toasted

MAKES 78 TO 80 (1-1/2-INCH SQUARE) COOKIES

Preheat oven to 350 degrees F. Cream the butter and sugar in the large bowl of an electric mixer until light and fluffy. Stir in egg yolks, flour, salt, and vanilla, mixing well. Spread dough out in a thin layer on an ungreased jellyroll sheet. Bake 20 to 25 minutes, until brown. Remove from oven and, while hot, sprinkle chocolate chips over crust and smooth with a spatula. Sprinkle with almonds. Cut into 1-1/2-inch squares while still warm.

# Turtle Bars

CRUST

2 cups sifted flour

1 cup firmly packed dark brown sugar

1/2 cup unsalted butter, at room temperature

1 cup whole pecans

NUT AND CHOCOLATE LAYER

2/3 cup unsalted butter

1/2 cup firmly packed dark brown sugar

1 cup milk chocolate or semi-sweet chocolate chips

MAKES 24 TO 30 BAR COOKIES

*For the crust:* Preheat oven to 350 degrees F. In a large bowl, combine first three ingredients, blending well. Place dough into a 9 x 13-inch ungreased baking pan, pat firmly, and cover bottom evenly. Sprinkle with pecans.

*For the nut and chocolate layer:* In a heavy 1-quart saucepan over medium heat, combine butter and sugar. Cook and stir until surface begins to boil. Boil 1-1/2 minutes, stirring constantly. Pour mixture evenly over pecans and bake 18 to 22 minutes. Remove from oven; while still warm, sprinkle with chocolate chips. Allow chips to melt slightly and then swirl, leaving some whole.

# Date Delights

1 cup sugar

1-1/2 cups pitted, chopped dates

1/2 cup butter

1 egg, beaten

2 cups crispy rice cereal

1 (7-ounce) package shredded sweet coconut, divided

1/2 teaspoon vanilla

MAKES ABOUT 48 FINGERS

Combine sugar, dates, butter, and egg in the top of a double boiler. Place over hot, simmering water and cook, stirring often, for 6 minutes. Remove from heat and transfer to a large bowl.

Stir in cereal, half the coconut, and vanilla. When the mixture has cooled enough to touch, scoop out one tablespoon of the mixture at a time and then roll or shape it into a finger shape. Roll each finger in remaining shredded coconut. Store cooled cookies in a covered container. These cookies freeze well.

# Twin Nut Finger Cookies

1/2 cup unsalted butter

3 tablespoons confectioners' sugar

1 cup sifted cake flour

1 cup ground almonds

Semisweet chocolate, melted, for dipping

Pistachio nuts, finely chopped, for coating

MAKES 36 SMALL COOKIES

Preheat oven to 325 degrees F. Cream butter, sugar, flour, and almonds together on medium speed with an electric mixer until blended. Remove dough, wrap in plastic wrap, and chill for 1 hour.

Roll a small amount of dough into a finger 1-1/2 to 2 inches long. Place fingers on ungreased baking sheets. Bake for 15 minutes; cool. Dip one end into melted chocolate and then into chopped pistachio nuts. Store in a covered container.

# Chocolate-Dipped Anise Biscotti

1-1/2 cups flour

1 teaspoon aniseed

1/2 teaspoon baking soda

1/4 teaspoon salt

3/4 cup sugar

2 tablespoons butter, at room temperature

2 large eggs

3 ounces premium dark chocolate, coarsely chopped

MAKES 22 BISCOTTI

Preheat oven to 350 degrees F. Lightly spoon flour into measuring cups; level with a knife. Combine flour, aniseed, baking soda, and salt, stirring well with a whisk. Place sugar and butter in a large bowl; beat at medium speed with a mixer until blended, about 2 minutes. Add eggs, one at a time, beating well after each addition. Add flour mixture to sugar mixture, beating just until blended. Turn dough out onto a lightly floured surface and knead lightly 7 times. Shape the dough into a 12-inch long roll. Place roll on a baking sheet coated with cooking spray; pat to 1-inch thickness. Bake for 40 minutes. Remove roll from baking sheet; cool 10 minutes on a wire rack.

Reduce oven temperature to 300 degrees F. Cut roll crosswise into 22 slices. Place, cut sides down, on the baking sheet. Bake for 10 minutes. Turn cookies over; bake an additional 10 minutes (cookies will be slightly soft in the center but will harden as they cool). Cool cookies completely on a wire rack.

Heat chocolate in a small heavy saucepan over low heat for 5 minutes, or until melted; stir until smooth. Dip cookies, top sides down, in chocolate; allow excess chocolate to drip into saucepan. Place cookies, chocolate sides up, on a rack set over a baking sheet. Let stand 1 hour until set.

*Bake the biscotti up to one week ahead and store in an airtight container. Biscotti can also be baked, but not dipped in chocolate, and frozen up to a month ahead. To serve, thaw biscotti and then dip them in melted chocolate.*

# White Chocolate Lemon Biscotti

3/4 cup sugar

2 teaspoons grated lemon zest

1 teaspoon vanilla

1/4 teaspoon lemon extract

2 large eggs

1-2/3 cups flour

1/2 teaspoon baking soda

1/4 teaspoon salt

1 (6-ounce) bar premium white chocolate, chopped*

MAKES 48 BISCOTTI

Preheat oven to 300 degrees F. Place first five ingredients in a large bowl; beat with a mixer at medium speed until well blended. Lightly spoon flour into measuring cups; level with a knife. Combine flour, baking soda, and salt; gradually add to sugar mixture, beating until well blended. Stir in chocolate.

Turn dough out onto a baking sheet coated with cooking spray. Shape dough into 2 (12-inch-long) rolls; pat to 2-1/2 inches wide. Bake for 35 minutes. Remove rolls from baking sheet; cool 10 minutes on a wire rack.

Cut each roll diagonally into 24 (1/2-inch) slices. Place, cut sides down, on the baking sheet. Bake for 10 to 12 minutes. Turn cookies over; bake an additional 10 minutes. Remove from baking sheet; cool completely on wire rack. Cookies will harden as they cool.

*Use white chocolate that contains cocoa butter; white chocolate morsels have no cocoa butter.*

Victor Higgins (1884–1949), *Sleeping Model*, n.d. Oil on canvas, 37-1/2 x 23 in. Collection of New Mexico Museum of Arts. Bequest of Joan Higgins Reed, 1983. Photograph by Blair Clark.

# Chocolate-Dipped Almond Meringues

MERINGUES

4 large egg whites

1/4 teaspoon cream of tartar

1/4 teaspoon salt

1/2 cup sugar

1/4 teaspoon almond extract

2 ounces bittersweet chocolate, finely chopped

CHOCOLATE GLAZE

1/2 cup semisweet chocolate chips

MAKES 2 DOZEN MERINGUES

*For the meringues:* Preheat oven to 200 degrees F. Cover a baking sheet with parchment paper.

Beat egg whites with a mixer at high speed until foamy. Add cream of tartar and salt; beat until soft peaks form. Gradually add sugar, 1 tablespoon at a time, beating until stiff peaks form (do not over beat). Gently fold in almond extract and chopped chocolate. Drop batter by rounded tablespoons onto prepared baking sheet. Bake for 2 hours, or until dry. (Meringues are done when the surface is dry and can be removed from paper without sticking to fingers.) Turn oven off; leave meringues in oven 1 hour, or until cool and crisp. Remove from oven; carefully remove meringues from paper. Cool completely on a wire rack.

*For the glaze:* Place semisweet chocolate chips in the top of a double boiler over simmering water and heat until melted and smooth (or microwave in a microwave-safe bowl at 50 percent power for 30 seconds). Dip half of each meringue in chocolate. Place on a wire rack to dry. Store in an airtight container.

*When preparing these cookies, be careful not to overbeat the egg whites; properly stiff peaks will have the consistency of marshmallow cream.*

# Forgotten Cookies

2 extra-large egg whites, at room temperature

1/8 teaspoon salt

1/2 teaspoon vanilla

1/2 cup sugar

1 cup miniature semisweet chocolate chips

1 cup chopped pecans (optional)

MAKES ABOUT 36 COOKIES

Preheat oven to 300 degrees F. Put egg whites into the bowl of an electric mixer fitted with a whisk. Beat at medium-low speed until frothy, about 2 minutes. Add salt and slowly increase speed, beating until stiff (but not dry) peaks form, about 1-1/2 minutes. Reduce speed to medium, adding vanilla. Then gradually add sugar, a few tablespoons at a time, and continue beating until mixture is smooth and glossy, about 2 minutes.

Gently fold in chocolate chips (and nuts, if using) into the beaten egg whites with a spatula. Drop meringues by spoonfuls onto parchment-lined or Silpat-lined baking sheets about 1 inch apart. Bake for 30 minutes and then turn off oven and go to bed! Leave meringues in the oven to dry out until the oven is cool, 6 hours or overnight.

*Serve with ice cream or fruit. This is one recipe you will not forget!*

# Coconut-Cranberry Chews

1-1/2 cups unsalted butter, at room temperature

2 cups sugar

1 tablespoon grated orange zest

2 teaspoons vanilla

1 large egg

3-1/4 cups flour

1 teaspoon baking powder

1/4 teaspoon salt

1-1/2 cups dried cranberries

1-1/2 cups sweetened flaked dried coconut

MAKES ABOUT 60 COOKIES

Preheat oven to 350 degrees F. In a large bowl, with mixer on medium speed, beat butter, sugar, orange zest, and vanilla until smooth. Beat in egg until well blended.

In a medium bowl, mix flour, baking powder, and salt. Add to butter mixture, stirring to mix. Beat on low speed until dough comes together, about 5 minutes (if it is too crumbly, dough needs to be mixed longer). Mix in cranberries and coconut.

Shape dough into 1-inch balls and place 2 inches apart on buttered 12 x 15-inch baking sheets.

Bake for 11 to 15 minutes, or until edges of cookies just begin to brown. If baking two sheets at once, switch oven rack positions halfway through the baking time. Let cookies cool on sheets 5 minutes, and then transfer to racks to cool completely.

*If a chewier cookie is desired, shorten baking time; if a crisp cookie is preferred, lengthen baking time.*

# Chocolate-Dipped Sandwich Cookies

1-1/2 cups unsalted butter, at room temperature, divided

1 cup plus 4 tablespoons sugar, divided

1 large egg yolk

1 teaspoon vanilla

2 cups flour

2 cups confectioners' sugar

4 tablespoons fresh lemon juice

6 ounces semisweet chocolate

1 tablespoon salted butter

Multicolored nonpareils, chocolate sprinkles, or finely chopped nuts

MAKES 36 COOKIES

Beat 1 cup butter and 1 cup sugar with mixer at medium speed. Gradually add egg yolk, vanilla, and flour, and mix thoroughly. Wrap dough in plastic wrap and chill for 2 hours.

Preheat oven to 325 degrees F. Form 1-inch balls of dough. Place 2 inches apart on ungreased baking sheets. Dip the bottom of a small glass into remaining sugar and use it to flatten each ball to 1/8 inch thickness, making a cookie of about 1-1/4 inches in diameter. Bake 10 to 12 minutes until cookies are lightly golden with light brown edges. Transfer to wire racks to cool.

Cream confectioners' sugar and remaining butter with a mixer on medium speed until light and fluffy. Add lemon juice to taste. Spread a teaspoonful of the sugar-lemon mixture on the tops of half of the cooled, baked cookies. Place the remaining cookies on top, pressing gently to make a sandwich.

In the top of a double boiler over simmering water, heat chocolate and salted butter until just melted and smooth. Dip up to half of each cookie sandwich (edge down) into chocolate, then into nonpareils, chocolate sprinkles, or nuts. Place on wire racks to set. Store in a tightly covered container, layered between sheets of wax paper, or freeze until needed.

Anonymous artist, *The Holy Family*, c. 1960. Oaxaca, Mexico. Painted wood, 14-7/8 in. high. Alexander Girard Foundation Collection. Museum of International Folk Art. Photograph by Michael Monteaux. A.1979.3.102.

## Peanut Butter Cookies

1-1/2 cups plus 2 tablespoons sifted flour

1/2 teaspoon baking soda

1/4 teaspoon salt

1/2 cup unsalted butter

1/2 cup plus 2 tablespoons peanut butter, creamy or crunchy

2/3 cup plus 1 teaspoon sugar

1/2 cup plus 1 teaspoon lightly packed light brown sugar

1/2 teaspoon vanilla

1 large egg, at room temperature

MAKES 18 LARGE COOKIES

Mix flour, baking soda, and salt together; set aside. Place butter, peanut butter, and sugars in the bowl of an electric mixer; cream until light and fluffy. Add vanilla and egg and mix until blended. Add dry ingredients and combine well. Wrap dough in plastic wrap and chill for several hours.

Preheat oven to 350 degrees F. Form small balls of dough and place 2 inches apart on a greased baking sheet. Bake about 15 minutes, or until golden brown around the edges and puffy and light in the center. Cool on the baking sheet.

# Orange Biscochitos

2 cups flour

1 teaspoon baking powder

1/4 teaspoon salt

3/4 cup plus 2 tablespoons sugar, divided

1/2 cup unsalted butter, at room temperature

1 large egg

1 tablespoon finely grated orange zest

1-1/2 teaspoons anise

1 teaspoon vanilla

1/4 cup confectioners' sugar

1/4 teaspoon ground cinnamon

Lightly spoon flour into measuring cups; level with a knife. Combine flour, baking powder, and salt, stirring with a whisk; set aside.

Place 3/4 cup sugar and butter in a large bowl; beat with a mixer at medium-high speed until light and fluffy (about 2 minutes). Add egg; beat 1 minute until well blended. Add orange zest, aniseed, and vanilla, beating until well blended. Beating at low speed, gradually add flour mixture, 1/2 cup at a time. Beat just until a soft dough forms. Wrap dough in plastic wrap; chill at least 1 hour.

Preheat oven to 350 degrees F. Shape dough into a 10-inch log. Cut log crosswise into 4 equal portions. Working on a lightly floured surface, with 1 portion at a time (keep remaining dough logs chilled until needed), divide dough into 10 equal pieces. Roll each piece into a ball; place dough balls 1-1/2 inches apart on a baking sheet coated with cooking spray.

Place confectioners' sugar in a small bowl. Dip bottom of a glass in confectioners' sugar; flatten dough ball with the bottom of the glass into a 2-inch circle. Repeat procedure with confectioners' sugar and remaining 9 dough balls.

Combine 2 tablespoons sugar and cinnamon. Sprinkle 10 dough circles evenly with 1-1/2 teaspoons cinnamon mixture. Bake for 10 minutes, or until edges of cookies are lightly browned. Cool on baking sheets 5 minutes, then cool completely on a wire rack. Repeat procedure 3 times with remaining dough, confectioners' sugar, and cinnamon mixture.

*Biscochitos originated in New Mexico. Dough may be prepared in advance and refrigerated up to three days. Store baked cookies in an airtight container for up to three days.*

# Mexican Butter Cookies

4-1/2 cups flour

1/2 teaspoon baking powder

1/4 teaspoon salt

2 cups butter, at room temperature

2 cups finely chopped walnuts

1 teaspoon vanilla

1 cup confectioners' sugar

Preheat oven to 350 degrees F. Sift flour, baking powder, and salt into a large bowl. Mix in butter until mixture forms a soft dough. Add nuts and vanilla and mix well. Shape dough into 1-inch balls and place on a baking sheet. Bake about 15 minutes, or until set. Let cool slightly. Roll in confectioners' sugar. Store the cookies in an airtight container.

# Pecan Tassies

1 (3-ounce) package cream cheese, at room temperature

1/2 cup unsalted butter, at room temperature

1 cup sifted flour

FILLING

1 large egg

3/4 cup firmly packed light brown sugar

1 tablespoon unsalted butter, at room temperature

Pinch of salt

1 teaspoon vanilla

2/3 cup coarsely chopped pecans

MAKES 24 BITE-SIZE TARTS

*For the shell:* Beat cream cheese and butter together in a medium bowl. Stir in flour and blend well. Cover bowl and chill dough mixture at least 1 hour.

Preheat oven to 325 degrees F. Form dough into two dozen 1-inch balls. Press into tiny muffin tins, shaping gently to bottom and sides.

*For the filling:* Beat together egg, sugar, butter, salt, and vanilla. Place half of pecans in pastry shells, add filling and then top with remaining pecans. Bake for 20 to 25 minutes, or until golden brown. Cool. Run a sharp knife around tins to remove tarts.

# German Anise Cookies

3 large eggs

1 cup sugar

1/4 cup anise oil*

1-1/2 cups sifted flour

1/2 teaspoon salt

1 teaspoon baking powder

Colored or silver sprinkles, optional

MAKES 36 SMALL COOKIES

Beat eggs until thick. Gradually add sugar and continue beating for 1 minute. Add anise oil and mix well. Add flour, salt, and baking powder, blending until incorporated. Drop dough from teaspoon 1 inch apart on greased baking sheet. Decorate with colored or silver sprinkles, if desired. Let stand refrigerated overnight.

Preheat oven to 325 degrees F. Bake cookies 15 minutes, until very light brown. Cool on wire racks. Store the cookies in a covered container.

*\*Anise oil is available at the pharmacy.*

Anonymous artist, *The Tree of Life*, c. 1962. Kurpie Region, Poland. Cut paper, 9-3/4 x 4-1/2 in. Alexander Girard Foundation Collection. Museum of International Folk Art. Photograph by Michael Monteaux. A.1981.3.445.

# Snowy Peaks and Frosty Treats

❄

## Coffee Surprise

1 pint coffee ice cream

8 ounces brandy

6 chilled champagne or martini glasses

SERVES 6

Place ice cream and brandy in a chilled blender. Process to desired consistency. Pour into chilled glasses.

## Key Lime Coconut Snowballs

2/3 cup graham cracker crumbs

6 tablespoons fat-free sweetened condensed milk

1 teaspoon grated Key lime zest

1-1/2 tablespoons fresh Key lime juice

1 teaspoon vanilla

1 cup shredded unsweetened coconut, divided

1-1/4 cups confectioners' sugar

MAKES 24 SNOWBALLS

Combine crumbs, condensed milk, zest, juice, and vanilla in a medium bowl.

Add 2/3 cup coconut and beat with a mixer at medium speed for 1 minute, or until no longer grainy. Add sugar, 1/4 cup at a time, beating until well combined. Cover and chill 20 minutes.

Shape crumb mixture into 24 balls, about 1 teaspoon each. Place remaining 1/3 cup coconut in a shallow bowl and roll balls in coconut. Refrigerate balls in an airtight container for up to one day.

*Use regular limes if Key limes are not available. Unsweetened coconut is often labeled "desiccated" or "pulverized," and is often sold in health food stores.*

John Sloan (1871–1951), *Under the Old Portal*, 1919. Oil on canvas, 24 x 20 in. Collection of New Mexico Museum of Art. Gift of Julius Gans, 1946. Photograph by Blair Clark.

# Tia Josefina's Venezuelan Dessert
## (*Postre de Almendras*)

1-1/2 cups sugar

3/4 cup peeled, toasted almonds

1-1/4 cups unsalted butter, at room temperature

3 egg yolks

1 can sweetened condensed milk

24 ladyfingers

SUGAR SYRUP

3/4 cup water

1/2 cup sugar

1 tablespoon brandy or rum, optional

SERVES 8

Caramelize sugar by heating it in a skillet over medium heat until light brown. Spread thinly on greased foil while hot. When cool, crush into small pieces. Chop almonds and mix with sugar.

Beat butter until creamy, then add egg yolks and condensed milk, beating until smooth. Spread a layer of this butter mixture into an 8-inch square pan.

*For the sugar syrup:* Combine water and sugar in a small pan. Boil until sugar dissolves. Add optional brandy or rum. Moisten ladyfingers in sugar syrup, but don't let them get soggy.

Place one layer of ladyfingers in pan. Cover with a layer of butter mixture, gently pushing between ladyfingers, then sprinkle with almond mixture. Add next layer of ladyfingers, then butter mixture, finishing with almond mixture as topping.

Refrigerate several hours. *Buen Provecho!*

*Use ultra-pasteurized eggs as eggs in this recipe are not thoroughly cooked.*

# Natillas from the Santa Fe School of Cooking

4 eggs, separated

1/4 cup flour

1 quart heavy cream, divided

3/4 cup sugar

1/8 teaspoon salt

1/2 teaspoon vanilla

Cinnamon or nutmeg to garnish

SERVES 8 TO 10

Make a paste of egg yolks, flour, and 1/2 cup of the heavy cream. Add sugar and salt to the rest of the cream and scald in a saucepan. Gradually stir scalded cream into egg mixture and place in a double boiler.

Cook slowly, stirring constantly, until the mixture has thickened, about 20 minutes. Mix in vanilla and let cool. Beat egg whites until stiff, fold into custard. Pour into dessert bowls and garnish with cinnamon or nutmeg.

*In a hurry? Chill down over a bowl of ice.*

—*The Santa Fe School of Cooking*

# Frozen Mango, Blackberry Cassis, and Vanilla Mosaic

2 pints mango sorbet

1 pint vanilla ice cream

6 ounces fresh blackberries

1/4 cup sugar

2 tablespoons crème de cassis (black current liqueur), plus more for garnish

SERVES 10 TO 12

Place sorbet and ice cream in refrigerator until evenly softened, 45 minutes to 1 hour.

Meanwhile, purée blackberries, sugar, and cassis in a blender until smooth. Strain through a fine mesh sieve set over a bowl, pressing on and then discarding the solids. Freeze to thicken slightly, about 20 to 40 minutes, then stir until smooth.

Lightly oil a 9 x 5 x 3-inch loaf pan or other 7- to 8-cup capacity mold. Cut a piece of parchment to fit bottom and long sides of pan, leaving at least 3 inches of overhang on each side.

Fill pan decoratively with spoonfuls of sorbet and ice cream, pressing down and filling empty spaces with blackberry purée as you go. Smooth top, pressing down with back of the spoon to eliminate air spaces, then fold parchment flaps over top and freeze until solid, at least 3 hours.

To unmold, run a thin knife along the short sides of the pan to loosen mosaic and then open parchment and invert on a flat serving dish, discarding parchment. Slice mosaic into 1/2- to 3/4-inch-thick slices.

Garnish with fresh mint and a teaspoon of crème de cassis. May be made 5 days ahead and frozen, covered with plastic wrap.

# Cranberry Sorbet

1 (12-ounce) bag cranberries

3-1/2 cups water

2-1/2 cups sugar

Juice of one lemon

1 cup heavy whipping cream

SERVES 4 TO 6

Boil cranberries in water until berries pop, about 15 minutes. Push through sieve to strain. While warm, stir in sugar and lemon juice. Freeze until mushy.

Whip cream and stir into cranberry mixture. Refreeze.

# Apricot Soufflé with Caramel Almonds

11 ounces dried apricots

1/2 cup plus 1 teaspoon water, divided

1 cup almonds

6 tablespoons firmly packed brown sugar

1 cup apricot liqueur

1/2 cup heavy cream, whipped

2 egg whites, beaten to stiff peaks

SERVES 4 TO 6

Soak the apricots in 1/2 cup water for 4 to 6 hours.

Place almonds on a well-buttered baking sheet. Boil brown sugar with 1 teaspoon water, without stirring, until the mixture is caramel brown. Pour this mixture over the almonds and mix. Leave to set, forming a toffee brittle.

When the toffee is hard, place it between two tea towels and carefully hammer to break up the nuts; try not to squash them.

Drain the apricots, discarding the water. Purée the apricots with the liqueur in a food processor or blender until smooth. Fold in the whipped cream, and then carefully fold in the beaten egg whites. Pour into a serving bowl and chill.

Just before serving, mix half the nuts into the soufflé and sprinkle the remaining nuts over the top.

*Individual soufflé dishes can be used in place of one large bowl.*

# Frozen Biscuit Tortoni

3/4 cup heavy cream

3/4 cup crushed amaretti Italian cookies

1/4 cup sifted confectioners' sugar

Pinch of salt

1 teaspoon vanilla

Toasted salt-free almonds and candied fruit for garnish

SERVES 12

Whip heavy cream to soft peaks. Combine the cookies, sugar, and salt in a large bowl. Fold whipped cream and vanilla into crumb mixture. Divide among 12 paper muffin cups set in a muffin tin. Freeze.

Decorate with almonds and/or candied fruit.

May be kept covered in the freezer for two days before serving.

Edward Kemp, *La Bajada Hill near Santa Fe*, c. 1910–1920. Collection of the Palace of the Governors Photo Archives.

## Lemon Curd Mousse with Toasted Coconut and Blueberries

2 teaspoons water

1/2 teaspoon unflavored gelatin

1 cup sugar

1/2 cup fresh lemon juice

6 large egg yolks

2 tablespoons grated lemon zest

3/4 cup unsalted butter, cut into small pieces

1 cup sweetened flaked coconut

1/4 cup firmly packed golden brown sugar

1-1/2 cups chilled whipping cream

2 (6-ounce) baskets fresh blueberries

SERVES 4 TO 6

Place water in a small bowl; sprinkle gelatin over. Let stand 10 minutes.

Whisk sugar, lemon juice, yolks, and zest in a heavy medium saucepan to blend. Add butter; stir constantly over medium heat until mixture thickens and just begins to bubble at the edges, about 9 minutes. Remove from heat. Add gelatin mixture; stir to dissolve. Transfer lemon curd to a medium bowl. Press plastic wrap directly onto the surface.

Chill until cold. Can be made 3 days ahead. Keep chilled.

Preheat oven to 350 degrees F. Spread coconut on a baking sheet. Sprinkle brown sugar over coconut. Bake until coconut is golden, stirring occasionally, about 10 minutes. Cool.

Beat cream in a medium bowl until stiff peaks form. Fold whipped cream and half the coconut into the lemon curd to make a mousse.

On individual serving plates, place a scoop of mousse. Then layer 3 tablespoons berries, 3 tablespoons mousse, and sprinkle with coconut.

# Pumpkin Chai Pots de Crème

1 cup whipping cream

1 cup whole milk

1/4 cup firmly packed brown sugar

7 large egg yolks

1/4 cup granulated sugar

1/2 cup canned or cooked pumpkin

1/3 cup chai tea concentrate, or strong brewed chai tea

2 teaspoons grated orange or Meyer lemon zest

1 teaspoon vanilla

PUMPKIN SEED BRITTLE

1/3 cup sugar

1/4 cup water

1/2 cup hulled and roasted pumpkin seeds (sometimes sold as pepitas)

SERVES 6

Preheat oven to 325 degrees F (convection oven not recommended).

In a 2- to 3-quart pan over medium heat, stir cream, milk, and brown sugar until sugar is dissolved, 2 to 4 minutes. Remove from heat.

In a bowl, whisk egg yolks until light yellow. Add granulated sugar and whisk until blended. Gradually whisk a fourth of the hot cream mixture into the egg mixture. Then slowly whisk in remaining cream mixture and the pumpkin, chai, zest, and vanilla.

Divide mixture among six (3/4-cup) ramekins. Set pan in oven and pour in boiling water to halfway up the sides of ramekins.

Bake until custards barely jiggle when gently shaken, 45 to 50 minutes. Lift ramekins out of the water and let cool on racks for 30 minutes; then chill until cold, at least one hour. Cover when cold.

*For the brittle:* In a heavy 6- to 8-inch frying pan over medium-high heat, stir sugar and water until sugar is dissolved, 1 to 2 minutes. Cook without stirring, shaking pan often, until mixture is a deep amber color, 5 to 10 minutes. Remove from heat and stir in hulled roasted pumpkin seeds. Pour onto a 12 x 15-inch piece of buttered foil and spread thin. Let cool until hard, 6 to 10 minutes. Cut or break brittle into about 1/2-inch shards. Store airtight, if not using at once.

Garnish pots de crème with shards of pumpkin seed brittle. Custards and pumpkin seed brittle may be made up to 1 day ahead. Cover and chill custards; store brittle airtight at room temperature.

# Sorbet and Ice Cream Terrine with Blackberry Compote

1 pint raspberry sorbet

1 pint lemon sorbet

1 pint vanilla ice cream

1 pint mango sorbet

1 pint boysenberry sorbet

COMPOTE

1/2 cup seedless blackberry jam

2 teaspoons grated lemon zest

1 teaspoon fresh lemon juice

2 (1/2-pint) containers fresh blackberries

1 tablespoon thinly sliced fresh mint leaves

SERVES 10

*For the terrine*: Line 9 x 5 x 3-inch metal loaf pan with 2 layers of plastic wrap, extending 3 inches over the sides. Scoop raspberry sorbet into medium bowl and stir to soften; let stand at room temperature until sorbet is spreadable, stirring occasionally, about 10 minutes. Spread sorbet evenly in the bottom of prepared loaf pan. Place loaf pan in freezer.

Scoop lemon sorbet into another medium bowl; stir and let stand at room temperature until spreadable, stirring occasionally, about 10 minutes. Spoon lemon sorbet in large dollops atop raspberry sorbet, then spread in an even layer. Return loaf pan to freezer. Repeat procedure with vanilla ice cream, then mango sorbet, and finally boysenberry sorbet. Fold plastic wrap overhang over terrine; cover with aluminum foil. Freeze terrine overnight. Terrine can be made 4 days ahead. Keep frozen.

*For the compote*: Stir jam in heavy medium saucepan over medium-low heat until melted. Stir in lemon zest and juice. Cool to room temperature. Stir in blackberries, crushing some with a fork to release juices. Refrigerate compote until cold, at least 2 hours and up to 1 day.

Stir sliced mint into blackberry compote. Invert terrine onto platter; peel off plastic wrap. Cut terrine into slices. Serve with blackberry compote.

# Cherries Jubilee Ice Cream Pie

CHERRY SAUCE

1/3 cup water

1/4 cup sugar

1 tablespoon cornstarch

2 tablespoons brandy

1 (12-ounce) package frozen pitted dark sweet cherries

CRUST

2 tablespoons butter, melted

2 tablespoons honey

1-1/2 cups graham cracker crumbs (about 9 cookie sheets)

4 cups vanilla low-fat ice cream, softened

SERVES 8

Preheat oven to 375 degrees F.

*For the cherry sauce*: Combine first 5 ingredients in a medium saucepan. Bring to a boil and cook 2 minutes, or until thick, stirring constantly. Cool completely.

*For the crust*: Combine butter and honey in a medium bowl. Add graham cracker crumbs, stirring to blend. Press mixture into the bottom and up the sides of a 9-inch pie plate. Bake at 375 degrees F for 8 minutes. Cool completely.

Place 1/2 cup cooled cherry mixture in a food processor; process until smooth. Place the remaining cherry mixture in an airtight container. Cover and chill.

Place ice cream in a large bowl and beat with a mixer at medium speed until smooth. Add puréed cherry mixture, and gently fold in to achieve a swirl pattern. Spoon mixture into the cooled crust. Cover and freeze 4 hours, or until firm. Top with reserved cherry sauce just before serving.

Anonymous artist, *Guardian Angel*, c. 1960. Kuna people, San Blas Islands, Panama. Appliquéd, embroidered cotton, 16-3/4 x 19-1/2 in. Alexander Girard Foundation Collection. Museum of International Folk Art. Photograph by Michael Monteaux. A.1979.67.678.

## Cranberry Refrigerator Cake

2 cups chopped fresh cranberries

1 large banana, diced

2/3 cup sugar

2 cups crushed vanilla wafers, divided

1/2 cup butter

1 cup confectioners' sugar

2 eggs

1/2 cup chopped walnuts

1 cup whipping cream, whipped

SERVES 8 TO 10

Mix together cranberries, banana, and sugar; set aside. Place half of the crushed wafers in the bottom of an 8 x 8 x 2-inch pan.

Cream butter and confectioners' sugar together. Add eggs and beat well. Spread this mixture over the crumbs.

Top with a layer of the cranberry-banana mixture and sprinkle with the chopped nuts. Spread whipped cream over top. Cover with remaining wafers and chill overnight.

*Use ultra-pasteurized eggs as eggs in this recipe are not thoroughly cooked.*

# Lemon Meringue Ice Cream
## in Toasted Pecan Crust

### LEMON CURD

2 large eggs

2 large egg yolks

6 tablespoons unsalted butter

1 cup sugar

6 tablespoons fresh lemon juice

2 teaspoons finely grated
   lemon zest

Pinch of salt

### CRUST

1-1/2 cups finely chopped pecans
   or almonds

1/4 cup sugar

1/4 cup butter, melted

3 cups vanilla ice cream, slightly
   softened, divided

### MERINGUE

4 large egg whites, at room temperature

Pinch of cream of tartar

6 tablespoons sugar

SERVES 8

*For the lemon curd*: Whisk eggs and yolks in a medium bowl. Melt butter in medium metal bowl set over a large saucepan of simmering water. Whisk in sugar, lemon juice, zest, and salt. Carefully whisk in egg mixture. Whisk until thermometer inserted into curd registers 178 to 180 degrees F, about 8 minutes. Transfer to a small bowl. Press plastic wrap on top of curd; chill 4 hours. Can be made 2 days ahead. Keep chilled.

*For the crust*: Preheat oven to 400 degrees F. Mix nuts, sugar, and butter in a medium bowl until moistened. Press mixture into the bottom and up the sides of a 9-inch diameter glass pie dish. (Mixture will be crumbly). Bake until crust is lightly toasted, about 12 minutes. (Crust will slip down the sides of dish.) Use the back of the spoon to press crust back into place. Cool on a rack. Freeze crust 30 minutes.

Dollop 1-1/2 cups ice cream over crust; spread into an even layer. Spread lemon curd over ice cream; freeze until firm, about 2 hours. Dollop 1-1/2 cups softened ice cream over lemon curd; spread into an even layer. Cover and freeze until firm, about 2 hours.

*For the meringue*: Using an electric mixer, beat egg whites in a medium bowl until frothy. Beat in cream of tartar. With mixer running, gradually add sugar. Beat until stiff peaks form. Spoon meringue over pie, spreading to seal at edges and swirling decoratively. Can be made 1 day ahead. Freeze pie.

Using a kitchen butane torch, toast meringue until golden in spots or place pie in a preheated 500 degrees F oven until meringue is golden in spots, watching to prevent burning, about 3 minutes. Cut pie into wedges; serve immediately.

# Amaretti Frozen Lemon Mousse
# with Blueberry Sauce

3 large eggs

3 large egg yolks

1/2 cup fresh lemon juice

1/2 cup sugar

1/4 cup unsalted butter, diced

3 teaspoons grated lemon zest

1 cup chilled whipping cream

1 cup crumbled amaretti cookies
  (about 24), divided

2 tablespoons butter

4 (1/2-pint) baskets blueberries

3/4 cup sugar

1 teaspoon cornstarch

Juice of 1 lemon

1 teaspoon grated lemon zest

**SERVES 10**

*For the mousse:* Line a 9-1/4 x 5-1/4 x 3-inch pan with plastic wrap, leaving a long overhang. Whisk eggs and yolks in a medium bowl to blend. Combine lemon juice, sugar, and butter in a heavy medium saucepan. Stir over medium heat until butter melts and sugar dissolves. Gradually whisk warm lemon mixture into eggs; return to saucepan. Stir over medium heat until custard thickens, about 3 minutes (do not boil). Transfer to a large bowl; whisk in zest. Chill lemon custard until cold, about 30 minutes.

Beat whipping cream in a medium bowl until peaks form. Fold whipped cream into lemon custard in 2 additions. Spread 1/4 of lemon mousse (about 1-1/2 cups) over the bottom of prepared pan. Sprinkle with 1/4 cup cookie crumbs. Repeat layering with lemon mousse and crumbs 2 more times. Top with remaining 1/4 of lemon mousse. Sprinkle with remaining 1/4 cup crumbs. Fold plastic wrap overhang over dessert to cover completely. Freeze dessert until solid (at least 6 hours).

*For the blueberry sauce:* Combine the butter, blueberries, sugar, cornstarch, lemon juice, and zest in a small pot over medium-high heat. Bring up to a low boil and stir gently until the berries break down and release their natural juices. The consistency should remain a bit chunky. Cool and store in the refrigerator until ready to serve. It will thicken when it cools slightly.

Unmold the mousse and cut in 1/2- to 3/4-inch slices. Spoon Blueberry Sauce over individual servings.

Jadwig Lukawska, *Domestic Scene*, c. 1962. Lowic Poland. Cut paper, 9-3/4 x 19-3/4 in. Alexander Girard Foundation Collection. Museum of International Folk Art. Photograph by Michael Monteaux. A.1981.3.354.

## Cold Pumpkin Soufflé

I envelope unflavored gelatin

1/4 cup rum

4 eggs

2/3 cup sugar

I cup cooked or canned pumpkin

1/2 teaspoon cinnamon

1/2 teaspoon ginger

1/4 teaspoon mace

1/4 teaspoon ground cloves

I cup whipping cream

SERVES 4

Sprinkle gelatin over rum to soften. Set over simmering water until gelatin is completely dissolved. Beat eggs thoroughly, gradually adding sugar. Beat until smooth and thick. Stir in pumpkin, spices, and rum mixture.

Whip cream; fold into pumpkin mixture. Fill a l-quart soufflé dish or individual soufflé dishes with mixture; chill until set.

Garnish servings with sweetened whipped cream and salted toasted pecans.
*Use ultra-pasteurized eggs as eggs in this recipe are not thoroughly cooked.*

## Chocolate and Peppermint Candy Ice Cream Sandwiches

I pint vanilla ice cream, softened slightly

1/4 teaspoon pure peppermint extract

I cup finely crushed peppermint hard candies (1/4 pound), divided

16 chocolate wafers

SERVES 8

Stir together ice cream (reserve ice cream pint container), extract, and 1/2 cup crushed candy in a bowl until combined. Transfer mixture to pint container and freeze until just firm enough to scoop, about 1 hour.

Working very quickly with a 1/4-cup ice cream scoop, scoop ice cream onto flat sides of 8 wafers (1 scoop per wafer), and then top with remaining 8 wafers, flat sides down. Place prepared sandwiches in a chilled baking sheet. Cover tightly with plastic wrap and freeze until firm, about 1 hour.

Unwrap sandwiches and roll edges in remaining 1/2 cup crushed candy. Rewrap and freeze until firm, about 1 hour.

Ice cream sandwiches keep 3 days.

# Pistachio Bonbons

1 pint pistachio ice cream, just soft enough to scoop

8 ounces bittersweet chocolate, coarsely chopped

2 tablespoons chopped pistachios

SERVES 4

Line a baking sheet or plate with parchment or waxed paper and place in the freezer for at least 15 minutes. Using an ice-cream scoop to shape, place 8 round scoops of ice cream (about 1/4 cup each) on baking sheet; freeze until firm, at least 30 minutes.

Place chocolate in a medium heatproof bowl set over (not in) a saucepan of simmering water. Stir frequently, until almost melted. Remove from heat, and stir until completely melted. Spoon 1 heaping tablespoon of warm melted chocolate on 1 scoop of ice cream. Using the bottom of a spoon, spread chocolate over and around the sides; sprinkle with pistachios. Working quickly, repeat with remaining scoops. Freeze until firm, at least 5 minutes.

Serve, or cover in plastic wrap and freeze up to 2 weeks.

# Mango and Macadamia Nut Ice Cream with Kiwi Coulis

1-1/2 quarts vanilla ice cream

1 cup unsalted macadamia nuts, chopped roughly

MANGO ICE CREAM

3 ripe mangoes or 2 cups canned mango purée

2 tablespoons sugar, or to taste

2/3 cup water

2 teaspoons lemon juice

1 tablespoon chopped preserved ginger

1-1/4 cups cream

Pinch of salt

KIWI COULIS

4 kiwis, peeled and chopped roughly

Kirsch to taste

Sugar to taste

SERVES 6

Soften the vanilla ice cream for about 10 minutes in the refrigerator. Place in a large bowl and beat in the nuts. Spoon the mixture into a wet 6-cup mold, working well up the side and leaving a hollow in the center for the mango ice cream. Cover and freeze for 30 minutes.

*For the mango ice cream*: Purée the fresh mangoes to give 2 cups. Strain the purée. Boil the sugar and water together for 10 minutes, then allow to cool. Add the mango, lemon juice, and ginger. Spoon into a container, cover, and freeze until hard around the edge. Transfer to a bowl and beat. Whip the cream and salt until stiff, and fold into the frozen mango mixture. Return to the freezer until the ice cream is almost firm. Beat again, and then spoon into the middle of the ice cream mold. Cover and freeze until ready to serve.

*For the coulis*: Purée the chopped kiwi. Add the Kirsch and sugar to taste. Strain the coulis if desired.

To serve, unmold the ice cream onto a serving platter. Garnish with chopped macadamia nuts and kiwi slices. Serve with the Kiwi Coulis.

# Cardamom-Pistachio Ice Cream

I (12-ounce) can evaporated milk, chilled

I (14-ounce) can sweetened condensed milk, chilled

I cup unsalted roasted pistachios

1/2 teaspoon ground cardamom

2 cups whipping cream

Strawberry syrup or whole strawberries for garnish

MAKES ABOUT 7-1/4 CUPS

In a blender, combine milks, pistachios, and cardamom; whirl until nuts are finely ground. In a large bowl with a mixer at high speed, whip cream until it holds distinct peaks. Add nut mixture to cream; fold to blend well.

Pour into a 2-quart (or larger) ice cream maker. Freeze according to manufacturer's directions until mixture is firm enough to scoop, dasher is hard to turn, or machine stops.

Scoop softly frozen ice cream into bowls.

Garnish with strawberry syrup and/or whole strawberries. Ice cream can be frozen up to one week in an airtight container.

# Lime Ice Cream with Caramelized Green Chile

LIME ICE CREAM

2 cups heavy cream

I cup milk

I cup sugar

Zest of 2 limes

1/2 cup freshly squeezed lime juice

1/4 cup Key lime juice (bottled is fine)

CARAMELIZED GREEN CHILE

6 green chiles, roasted, peeled, seeded, and rinsed

1/2 cup sugar

2 tablespoons water

1/4 teaspoon salt

MAKES I QUART

*For the lime ice cream*: Whisk together cream, milk, sugar, and zest. Quickly stir in lime juice and pour into ice cream maker. Freeze according to manufacturer's instructions.

*For the caramelized chile*: Blot chiles dry with paper towels and cut them into 1/4-inch strips. In a heavy bottomed saucepan, combine chiles, sugar, water, and salt. Cook over medium heat, stirring occasionally, until mixture thickens and becomes syrupy, about 12 minutes.

Remove from heat and strain chiles through a sieve. Scatter chiles on a lightly oiled plate and freeze. Add to Lime Ice Cream before storing in the freezer, or place a few pieces on top of each serving.

*The caramelized green chiles taste like pineapple—with a kick!*

*—John Vollertsen, Director, Las Cosas Cooking School, and restaurant critic*

Edward Kemp, *Patio of La Fonda Hotel*, Santa Fe, c. 1910–1920. Collection of the Palace of the Governors Photo Archives.

# Red, White, and Blueberry Ice Cream Sundaes

1 cup plus 2 (1/2-pint) containers blueberries, divided

2 teaspoons fresh lemon juice

2 cups confectioners' sugar

1 cup whipping cream

1/4 cup water

3/4 cup chilled whipping cream

1 pint vanilla ice cream

1 pint raspberry sorbet

1 pint strawberry ice cream

1/2 cup pecans, toasted and chopped

SERVES 6

Combine 1 cup blueberries and lemon juice in a medium bowl; mash well and set aside.

Sift confectioners' sugar into a heavy medium nonstick skillet. Cook over medium heat until sugar begins to dissolve, stirring occasionally, about 5 minutes. Continue to cook until syrup turns deep golden brown, stirring often, about 5 minutes longer.

Whisk in 1 cup cream and the water (mixture will bubble up). Reduce heat to medium-low, cover, and cook until most hard caramel bits dissolve, stirring occasionally, about 20 minutes. Remove from heat.

Stir in mashed blueberries; strain into a medium saucepan, pushing berries through. The blueberry mixture can be made 3 days ahead, covered and chilled.

To serve, rewarm blueberry sauce over low heat. Beat 3/4 cup cream in a medium bowl to soft peaks. Place 1 scoop each of vanilla ice cream, raspberry sorbet, and strawberry ice cream in each of 6 sundae dishes. Spoon warm blueberry sauce over ice creams. Garnish with remaining fresh blueberries, whipped cream, and pecans.

*These "patriotic" sundaes with their terrific blueberry caramel sauce are great fun for a Fourth of July party.*

# Maraschino Ice Cream Cake with Vanilla and Raspberry Sauces

## CAKE

6 egg yolks

1/4 cup plus 1 to 2 tablespoons maraschino liqueur, divided

3 tablespoons sugar

3 cups heavy cream

6 tablespoons confectioners' sugar, sifted

1-1/2 teaspoons vanilla

2 cups almond macaroons, crushed finely, divided

## VANILLA SAUCE

2 cups cream

2 eggs, beaten

2 egg yolks, beaten

1/2 cup sugar

1-1/2 teaspoons vanilla

## RASPBERRY SAUCE

1-1/2 pints raspberries, divided

2 cups water

1/2 to 1 cup sugar, according to taste

Toasted almonds and whole raspberries for garnish

SERVES 8

*For the cake*: Whisk the egg yolks with 1/4 cup liqueur and sugar until thick. Place the bowl over a pan of boiling water and continue to whisk the mixture until thick and creamy (a trail will be left on the mixture when the whisk is lifted). Place the bowl over ice and beat until cool.

In a separate chilled bowl, beat the cream until it holds soft peaks. Add the confectioners' sugar and vanilla and continue beating until well mixed. (Do not over beat.) Using a metal spoon, carefully fold the cream into the egg mixture. Chill in the freezer for 30 minutes.

Butter a 9-inch springform cake pan and pour in 1 cup of the almond macaroon crumbs. Pat down the crumbs firmly and evenly with the back of a spoon.

Remove the cream mixture from the freezer and stir. Pour 1/4 of the mixture over the crumbs and freeze for 15 minutes. Sprinkle 1/2 cup of the crumbs over the filling and sprinkle with some of the remaining maraschino liqueur. Return to the freezer for another 15 minutes. Add another quarter of the cream filling and continue layering the crumbs (with sprinkles of the maraschino liqueur if desired) and filling until you finish with a layer of cream filling on top. Be sure to freeze the cake for 15 minutes after adding a layer. When complete, cover and freeze the cake for at least 4 hours, or until thoroughly set.

*For the vanilla sauce*: Combine the cream, eggs, yolks, and sugar in a heavy bottomed saucepan and heat over low heat, stirring continuously with a wooden spoon until the mixture is thick enough to coat the back of the spoon. Remove from heat and beat in the vanilla. Cover and chill.

*For the raspberry sauce*: Place 1-1/2 cups raspberries in a saucepan with water and sugar to taste. Bring to a boil and boil, covered, for a few minutes. Be careful that the raspberries do not boil over. Remove the lid from the pan and continue to boil gently for 10 to 15 minutes, stirring occasionally. Remove the pan from the heat and allow to cool. Transfer the mixture to a food processor or blender and process until smooth. Reserve some whole berries for garnish. Stir in the remaining raspberries. Cover and chill.

To serve, remove the maraschino ice cream cake from the freezer 15 minutes before serving and turn out onto a serving platter. Decorate with almonds and whole raspberries. Pass the vanilla and raspberry sauces separately.

# Cold Lemon Soufflé

6 eggs, separated

1-1/2 cups sugar

Grated zest of 2 lemons

1 tablespoon unflavored gelatin

Juice of 3 lemons

1 pint whipping cream

SERVES 6 TO 8

Whisk egg yolks, then place in the top of a double boiler and combine with sugar and zest. Mix well. Cook 15 minutes, stirring occasionally.

Combine gelatin and lemon juice and warm over low heat until gelatin is dissolved. Add to egg yolk mixture. Cool.

Beat 6 egg whites until stiff peaks form. In a separate bowl, beat cream until soft peaks form. Fold egg whites and whipped cream into yolk mixture. Pour into an oiled 6-cup soufflé dish and chill.

# Frozen Lemon Soufflé

12 egg yolks

1-3/4 cups plus 2 teaspoons sugar, divided

3/4 cup lemon juice (from approximately 4 lemons)

Grated zest of 1 lemon

1/2 cup heavy cream

8 egg whites

Whipped cream and candied flowers for garnish, optional

SERVES 8

Select a skillet with deep sides into which a 2-quart bowl will fit comfortably. Add enough water to come up around the sides of the bowl without overflowing. Remove the bowl and start heating water in skillet.

In the 2-quart bowl, beat egg yolks and 1-1/2 cups sugar until mixture is light and lemon colored. Add the lemon juice and, when the water is boiling, set the bowl in the skillet and continue beating until the egg mixture is like a very thick, smooth, and creamy custard, about 10 minutes. The temperature of the egg mixture at this point should be about 120 to 140 degrees F.

Scrape the mixture into another mixing bowl and stir in the zest. Let cool and chill thoroughly.

Prepare a 5-cup soufflé dish. Tear off a length of wax paper that will fit around the outside of the soufflé dish, adding 1 or 2 inches for overlap. Fold the wax paper lengthwise into thirds. Wrap it around the outside of the soufflé dish about 2 inches above the rim, making sure that it overlaps itself at the ends by at least 1 inch. Secure it with string or paper clips.

Beat heavy cream, and when it starts to thicken, add 2 teaspoons sugar. Continue beating until stiff. Fold this into the chilled egg mixture.

In a separate bowl beat the egg whites. When they start to mound, add the remaining 1/4 cup of sugar, beating constantly. Continue beating until whites are stiff. Fold them into the soufflé mixture.

Pour the mixture into the prepared dish and place in the freezer. Freeze for several hours or overnight until completely frozen.

To serve, remove the wax paper. Garnish, if desired, with whipped cream, piped out of a pastry tube, and candied flowers.

Anonymous artist, *Basket*, c. 1965. Tamil Nadu, India. Woven palm leaf with foil, 6-1/2 in. high. Alexander Girard Foundation Collection. Museum of International Folk Art. Photograph by Michael Monteaux. A.1981.28.169V.

# Frozen Strawberry and Macaroon Parfaits

2 cups sliced hulled strawberries (about 12 ounces)

1 (10-ounce) package frozen strawberries in syrup, thawed

1-1/2 cups coarsely crushed Italian almond macaroons or crushed biscotti

1 pint vanilla frozen yogurt

4 fresh strawberries (optional)

SERVES 4

Mix fresh and thawed strawberries in a medium bowl. Divide half of strawberry mixture among four (10- to 12-ounce) goblets or wine glasses. Top with half of crushed macaroons and small scoops of frozen yogurt. Repeat layering. Freeze until ready to serve.

Garnish each parfait with 1 strawberry, if desired.

Gustave Baumann (1881–1971), *A Lilac Year*, n.d. Color woodcut, 12 x 13 in. Collection of New Mexico Museum of Art. Purchased with funds raised by School of American Research, 1952. Photograph by Blair Clark.

# Fruit Fiestas

## Gingered Peach Crisp

### FILLING

3-1/2 pounds ripe peaches, peeled, pitted, and sliced

2 tablespoons fresh lemon juice

1/3 cup firmly packed light brown sugar

1/4 cup sugar

1/4 cup chopped candied crystallized ginger

2 gingersnap cookies

Pinch of salt

### TOPPING

1 dozen gingersnap cookies

1 cup oats

3/4 cup pecans

1/2 cup firmly packed light brown sugar

1/2 teaspoon salt

1/4 cup butter, melted

**SERVES 8**

*For the filling*: Preheat oven to 375 degrees F. Butter a 9 x 13-inch baking dish. Mix the peaches with the lemon juice in a large bowl. Stir in the remaining filling ingredients and pour into the baking dish.

*For the topping*: Combine the gingersnaps, oats, pecans, sugar, and salt in a food processor. Add the butter and pulse until the mixture becomes a crumbly meal. Spoon over the peaches evenly, packing down lightly.

Bake for 40 to 45 minutes, until the topping is crunchy and the peaches are very tender. Serve warm, perhaps with a scoop of ice cream on the side.

—*Cheryl Alters Jamison, cookbook author from Santa Fe*

## Grilled Peaches with Sangria Syrup

### SYRUP

1 cup fruity red wine

1 (3-ounce) can orange juice concentrate

3 tablespoons Triple Sec (or other orange-flavored liqueur), divided

2 tablespoons brandy (or peach- or apricot-flavored brandy)

2 tablespoons sugar, divided

2-1/2 to 3 pounds firm but ripe peaches, peeled and halved

**SERVES 6**

*For the syrup:* Combine the wine, juice, 2 tablespoons Triple Sec, brandy, and 1 tablespoon sugar in a heavy saucepan. Bring the syrup to a boil over high heat; reduce to medium-low heat and simmer for about 5 minutes. Add the remaining Triple Sec and sugar, if needed. Continue simmering until reduced by about one-third.

Fire up the grill, bringing the temperature to medium.

Brush the peaches lightly with the syrup, reserving the remainder. Grill the peaches, cut side down, uncovered for 6 to 8 minutes, or as needed until softened with a few brown and caramelized edges. Brush with the remaining syrup in the last minute or so of grilling. Divide the peaches among bowls and serve.

# Peach and Pistachio Cobbler

## FILLING

1/2 cup sugar

2 tablespoons cornstarch

1/2 teaspoon ground cinnamon

1/4 teaspoon ground nutmeg

1/4 teaspoon salt

8 to 10 peaches, peeled, pitted, and sliced 1 inch thick

## TOPPING

2 cups flour

1/2 cup unsalted pistachios, finely chopped

1/4 cup plus 1 tablespoon sugar, divided

1/2 teaspoon salt

2 teaspoons baking powder

3/4 cup cold unsalted butter, cut into 1/2-inch cubes

3/4 cup whole milk

1/4 teaspoon cinnamon

Place rack in the lower third of the oven and preheat to 350 degrees F. Grease a 12-inch oval or 9 x 13-inch baking dish, 2-quart capacity.

*For the filling:* In a small bowl, stir together the sugar, cornstarch, cinnamon, nutmeg, and salt. Place the peaches in a large bowl, sprinkle with the sugar mixture, and toss to distribute evenly. Spread the peach mixture in the prepared baking dish and set aside while you prepare the topping.

*For the topping:* In a large bowl, mix together the flour, pistachios, 1/4 cup sugar, salt, and baking powder. Using a pastry blender, or your fingers, cut butter into the flour mixture until the texture resembles coarse cornmeal, leaving some pieces of butter about the size of small peas. Add milk; stir just until the mixture pulls together.

Pinch off chunks of the dough and place them on top of the peach mixture, covering it nearly completely. Or, on a lightly floured work surface, roll out the dough to the same dimensions as the baking dish and carefully lay it over the filling.

In a small bowl, mix together cinnamon and 1 tablespoon sugar and sprinkle the mixture on top of the dough. Bake until topping is firm and golden brown, and filling bubbles slowly, 45 to 60 minutes. Remove from oven and let cool for 30 minutes before serving.

Serve with a small scoop of vanilla ice cream or a splash of heavy cream.

# Pineapple Rings with Coconut Sorbet

1 large ripe pineapple, peeled (about 4 pounds)

4 tablespoons butter

1/4 cup firmly packed light brown sugar

2 tablespoons orange juice

Pinch of cinnamon

1 pint coconut sorbet

Toasted coconut, optional

Diced crystallized ginger, optional

Slice pineapple crosswise into 1/2-inch-thick rings. With a small, sharp knife, cut out the core from each slice. Set the rings aside.

In a small saucepan, melt butter over medium heat. Add sugar, orange juice, and cinnamon, stirring constantly with a wire whisk until sugar is melted and sauce begins to bubble. Remove from heat. Let sauce cool to room temperature before serving.

Heat grill. Grill pineapple rings 3 to 5 minutes per side, until edges are browning. To serve, divide pineapple rings among four bowls, pour brown sugar sauce over pineapple, and scoop coconut sorbet over top. Sprinkle with toasted coconut and crystallized ginger, if desired.

Anonymous artist, *Banks*, ca. 1960. San Pedro Tlaquepaque, Jalisco, Mexico. Painted earthenware. Alexander Girard Foundation Collection. Museum of International Folk Art. Photograph by Michael Monteaux. A.1979.5.3xxx.

## Rhubarb Strawberry Crisp

4 cups diced rhubarb

4 cups fresh strawberries, hulled and halved

I cup sugar, divided

2 teaspoons orange zest

2 tablespoons cornstarch

1/4 cup Grand Marnier (or Cointreau)

10 tablespoons cold unsalted butter, cut into 1/2-inch pieces, divided

1-1/4 cups flour

1/4 cup firmly packed light brown sugar

Pinch of salt

SERVES 6

Preheat oven to 375 degrees F. In a large bowl, combine the rhubarb, strawberries, 3/4 cup sugar, zest, cornstarch, and liqueur; mix well. Grease a 9 x 13-inch glass baking dish with 1 tablespoon butter and transfer the fruit mixture to the prepared dish.

In a mixing bowl, combine the remaining butter, flour, remaining sugar, brown sugar, and salt; cut together until mixture resembles coarse crumbs. Sprinkle topping evenly over the fruit and bake until topping is golden brown and crispy and fruit is bubbly, about 45 to 50 minutes. Cool briefly. Serve warm with a dollop of whipped cream, ice cream, or crème fraîche.

## Raspberry Sabayon

I large egg

8 egg yolks

I cup sugar

1-1/2 cups dry white wine

2 tablespoons raspberry brandy

I quart raspberries

SERVES 6 TO 8

With an electric mixer, beat egg, yolks, and sugar about 8 minutes; add white wine. Beat 2 minutes more at high speed. Transfer mixture to top of double boiler. Cook over high heat beating with wire whisk until thick. Add raspberry brandy and then whip 1 minute. Pour warm sauce into champagne glasses that have been filled with raspberries.

# Strawberry Margarita Crisp

2 tablespoons graham cracker
  crumbs

9 crispy coconut macaroons
  (about 1/4 pound)

2 tablespoons butter, melted

4 cups medium strawberries,
  stemmed and hulled

1/3 cup sugar

1/3 cup tequila

1 tablespoon cornstarch

1 tablespoon Triple Sec or other
  orange-flavored liqueur

1 tablespoon sliced almonds

Sliced strawberries, optional

SERVES 6

Preheat oven to 350 degrees F. Place graham cracker crumbs and maca-roons in a food processor; process until macaroons are finely ground. With food processor on, slowly pour butter through food chute and process until well blended.

Combine strawberries, sugar, tequila, cornstarch, and Triple Sec in a medium bowl; stir well. Spoon strawberry mixture into an 7 x 11-inch baking dish coated with cooking spray. Sprinkle with graham cracker–macaroon mixture and almonds. Bake for 25 minutes, or until sauce is thick and bubbly. Garnish with sliced strawberries, if desired.

*For an elegant presentation, serve in margarita glasses with rims dipped in water and then sugar.*

# Raspberry Fool

3 envelopes gelatin, softened

1/3 cup boiling water

1 pint raspberries

6 cups heavy cream

Sugar to taste

Brandy to taste

TOPPING

2 cups heavy cream

Sugar to taste

Brandy to taste

SERVES 8 TO 10

Dissolve the gelatin in boiling water, stirring thoroughly. Purée the raspberries (and their juice) in a blender or food processor. With the motor still running, add the dissolved gelatin in a steady stream.

Lightly whip the cream with the sugar, to taste; then add the brandy to taste. (Take care; if the brandy is added too soon, the cream will not thicken.) Care-fully fold in the raspberry purée. When thoroughly mixed, transfer to a glass serving bowl and refrigerate, overnight if possible.

*For the topping*: Whip the heavy cream with sugar, to taste. When thick, add brandy to taste and use the mixture to decorate the Raspberry Fool.

# Ginger Yogurt with Berries and Crunchy Caramel

BERRIES AND YOGURT

6 (7-ounce) containers plain
  Greek yogurt

1 (4-ounce) package crystallized
  ginger, minced (about 3/4 cup)

1 (1/2-pint) container raspberries

1 (1/2-pint) container blackberries

1 (1/2-pint) container blueberries

1 (1/2-pint) container strawberries,
  hulled, halved (quartered if large)

CARAMEL TOPPING

1 cup sugar

1/4 cup water

SERVES 6

*For the berries and yogurt*: Mix yogurt and ginger in a medium bowl. Spread berries in a large shallow serving bowl; cover berries with yogurt. Cover and chill. Can be made 4 hours ahead.

*For the caramel topping*: Stir sugar and water in a heavy medium saucepan over low heat until sugar dissolves. Increase heat; boil without stirring until mixture is a dark caramel color, swirling pan occasionally, about 7 minutes. Immediately pour hot caramel over berries and yogurt; avoid pouring down inner sides of bowl. Let stand until caramel hardens, about 5 minutes, and serve.

# Roasted Cherry Pavlova
## with Cinnamon Whipped Cream

MERINGUE CAKE

4 large egg whites

1 cup superfine sugar

1 teaspoon white vinegar

1/2 tablespoon cornstarch

TOPPING

1 pint whipping cream, chilled

1/8 teaspoon ground cinnamon

ROASTED CHERRIES

3 pounds fresh cherries, pitted

6 tablespoons sugar

6 tablespoons Armagnac brandy
 or cognac

6 tablespoons almond oil

1-1/2 vanilla beans, split lengthwise

SERVES 10 TO 12

*For the meringue cake*: Preheat oven to 250 degrees F and place rack in center of oven. Line a baking sheet with parchment paper and draw a 7-inch circle on the paper.

Beat egg whites on medium-high speed until they hold soft peaks. Start adding sugar, a tablespoon at a time, and continue to beat until the meringue holds very stiff peaks. (Test to see if the sugar is fully dissolved by rubbing a little of the meringue between your thumb and index finger. The meringue should feel smooth, not gritty. If it feels gritty the sugar has not fully dissolved so keep beating until it feels smooth between your fingers).

Sprinkle the vinegar and cornstarch over the top of the meringue and, with a rubber spatula, fold in. Gently spread the meringue inside the circle drawn on the parchment paper, smoothing the edges and making sure the edges of the meringue are slightly higher than the center. (You want a slight well in the center of the meringue to place the whipped cream and the fruit.) Bake for 1 hour 15 minutes, or until the outside is dry and takes on a very pale cream color. Turn off the oven, leave the door slightly ajar, and let the meringue cool completely in the oven. (The outside of the meringue will feel firm to the touch if gently pressed, but as it cools you will get a little cracking and you will see that the inside is soft and marshmallowy.)

The cooled meringue can be made and stored in a cool dry place, in an airtight container, for a few days.

*For the topping*: Place the cold cream and the cinnamon into a large bowl. Whip the cream until soft peaks form. Chill until ready for assembly.

*For the roasted cherries*: Heat the oven to 400 degrees F. In a large bowl, combine the cherries, sugar, brandy, and almond oil. Scrape seeds from the vanilla bean into the mixture and combine. Pour the mixture into a medium baking dish and bake until the cherries are slightly soft, about 8 minutes. Remove from the oven and allow to cool slightly before assembling the Pavlova.

When ready to assemble, place the cooled meringue cake onto a large platter. Mound the whipped cream in the center, then spoon the roasted cherries over the cream.

*This dessert was said to have originated in Australia or New Zealand in the 1920s and named in honor of the visiting Russian ballerina Anna Pavlova.*

Edward Kemp, *Isleta Indians meeting train*, c. 1910–1920. Collection of the Palace of the Governors Photo Archives.

# Danish Apple Surprise

FILLING

12 large Granny Smith apples

1/2 cup unsalted butter

TOPPING

1-1/4 cups unsalted butter

3/4 cup sugar

1 cup flour

1-1/2 cups sliced almonds

1 teaspoon cinnamon

Pinch of ground cloves

SAUCE

1/2 pint whipping cream

4 egg yolks

8 tablespoons sugar

1 teaspoon vanilla

SERVES 8

*For the filling:* Peel, core, and slice the apples; sauté in butter, in a pan without a lid, until cooked but still firm. Arrange apples in a well-greased 9-inch pie plate.

*For the topping:* Melt butter. Mix sugar, flour, almonds, cinnamon, and cloves in a bowl; add melted butter and mix well with a large spoon. With fingers, spread topping on the apples so they are completely covered. Bake at 350 degrees F for 40 minutes to 1 hour. (If topping turns too brown, cover lightly with foil.) Cool for at least an hour before serving.

*For the sauce:* Whip cream until firm, then refrigerate. In another bowl, whip egg yolks and sugar until thick; add vanilla. Carefully fold whipped cream into egg yolk mixture. Scoop into serving bowl and refrigerate until it is time to serve.

# Summer Fruit Clafouti

1-1/2 pounds apricots, pluots, or purple-skinned plums

1/4 cup sweet white wine (such as Muscat or late-harvest Riesling)

3 large eggs

1 cup milk

1/2 cup sugar

1/2 cup flour

5 tablespoons unsalted butter, melted

1 tablespoon vanilla

1/8 teaspoon salt

Confectioners' sugar

SERVES 8

Preheat oven to 325 degrees F. Butter a shallow 2-quart baking dish. Cut fruit off pits into 1/4-inch-thick wedges and drop into a bowl. Add wine and mix gently. Let stand 5 minutes.

In a blender, combine eggs, milk, sugar, flour, butter, vanilla, and salt; whirl until smooth. With a slotted spoon, transfer fruit to buttered baking dish. Pour the wine and juices from the fruit into the egg mixture and whirl again to blend. Pour egg mixture over fruit.

Bake clafouti in the upper third of preheated oven until puffed and set to the touch in the center, 55 to 65 minutes. Serve warm (clafouti will settle slightly as it cools). Sprinkle confectioners' sugar over the top just before serving.

*Clafouti is an old French dessert traditionally baked in late spring. Serve it warm with vanilla ice cream.*

# Cinnamon Roasted Pears with Dried Cherries and Caramel Sauce

6 ounces dried tart cherries

1/4 cup orange-flavor liqueur

6 tablespoons butter

1 teaspoon cinnamon

8 Bosc pears, peeled, halved lengthwise, and cored

CARAMEL SAUCE

1 cup firmly packed light brown sugar

1/4 cup sugar

1/2 cup light corn syrup

1 cup heavy cream

1/4 teaspoon salt

SERVES 8

Place cherries in a small bowl. Heat orange liqueur almost to boiling. Pour hot liqueur over cherries; set aside until liquid is absorbed.

Heat oven to 350 degrees F. In a small saucepan over low heat, melt butter, and then stir in cinnamon. Arrange pears, cut side up, in an ungreased 9 x 13-inch baking dish. Brush pears with some of the cinnamon butter, and spoon some softened cherries into each pear half. Bake pears, uncovered, 30 to 35 minutes, or until fork tender, brushing occasionally with cinnamon butter.

*For the caramel sauce:* In a medium saucepan over medium heat, combine sugars, corn syrup, cream, and salt. Heat to boiling, then reduce heat to low and cook until mixture reaches 225 degrees F on a candy thermometer, or until it forms a soft ball when a small amount is dropped into cold water.

To serve, spoon some warm caramel sauce onto a small plate. Arrange two pear halves on top of sauce and drizzle with a bit more sauce.

# Pears Poached in Red Wine

4 firm but ripe Bosc pears of uniform size

1 (750-ml) bottle fruity red wine (Merlot or Zinfandel)

3/4 cup sugar

1 strip lemon peel, 2 inches long and 1 inch wide

1 cinnamon stick, 2 to 3 inches long

2 whole cloves

2 tablespoons unsalted butter, at room temperature

SERVES 4

Peel pears, leaving the stems in place. Working from the bottom end, using an apple corer, remove the core from each pear, stopping within 1 inch of the stem end. Remove a thin slice from bottom of each pear so that it will stand upright.

Select a deep saucepan with a tight-fitting lid just large enough to accommodate pears. In the saucepan, combine the wine, sugar, peel, cinnamon stick, and cloves and stir to dissolve the sugar. Add the pears, standing them close to one another in the pan. If the pears are not covered by the wine, add just enough water to cover them completely.

Bring the mixture to a boil over medium heat, and then reduce the heat to maintain a slow, gentle simmer. Poach uncovered until the pears are tender when pierced with a skewer or cake tester, approximately 20 to 30 minutes. Using a slotted spoon, carefully remove the pears from the liquid. Let cool to room temperature and cover with plastic wrap.

Return the wine mixture to medium heat and simmer until it is reduced to 3/4 cup and has the consistency of thick syrup, 40 to 50 minutes.

To serve, add the butter to the hot syrup and swirl the mixture in the pan until the butter is melted. Divide the pears among individual shallow dessert bowls or deep plates. Pour an equal amount of the sauce over each pear and serve immediately.

# Campari-Poached Pears with Raspberry Sauce

2 cups cranberry-raspberry juice

1-1/4 cups sugar

1/2 cup Campari

3 (3 x 1-inch) strips orange peel

6 Bosc pears

1 lemon, cut in half

1 (10-ounce) package frozen raspberries in syrup, thawed

4 tablespoons orange liqueur, divided

2 tablespoons red currant jelly

1 cup mascarpone cheese

2 tablespoons confectioners' sugar

Fresh mint leaves for garnish

SERVES 6

Combine juice, sugar, Campari, and peel in a heavy large saucepan. Bring to a boil, stirring until sugar dissolves. Cover and reduce heat to very low, keeping the poaching liquid hot.

Peel pears, leaving stems attached. Rub pears all over with cut lemon halves. Using a melon baller, remove core through the wide end of the pears, then cut a thin slice off the wide ends so the pears can stand upright. Add pears to poaching liquid. Simmer uncovered over medium-low heat until pears are tender, turning occasionally, about 20 minutes. Cool pears in poaching liquid. Refrigerate until cold, at least 6 hours.

Purée raspberries with their syrup, 2 tablespoons liqueur, and currant jelly in a blender. Strain raspberry sauce through a fine sieve. Chill until cold, about 1 hour.

Whisk mascarpone, confectioners' sugar and remaining 2 tablespoons liqueur in a bowl to blend.

Spoon some raspberry sauce onto plates. Stand pears upright in center of sauce. Spoon dollops of the mascarpone mixture alongside.

Garnish with mint leaves.

Marianna Pietrzah, *Rooster*, 1962. Bledow, Lowicz, Poland. Cut paper, 4-1/4 x 4 in. Alexander Girard Foundation Collection. Museum of International Folk Art. Photograph by Michael Monteaux. A.1981.3.333.

# Summer Cherries Jubilee

1-1/2 cups pitted sweet cherries

1/4 cup cherry preserves

1/2 cup Cabernet Sauvignon, or other dry red wine

1 tablespoon amaretto liqueur

2 teaspoons fresh lemon juice

3 cups vanilla low-fat frozen yogurt

SERVES 4

Combine first three ingredients in a small saucepan and bring to a boil. Reduce heat and simmer 5 minutes, stirring frequently. Stir in amaretto and lemon juice.

Serve warm over frozen yogurt.

*A cherry pitter will save you preparation time and prevent a red-stained thumb.*

# Pears in Chocolate Sabayon

6 Bartlett pears

3 cups water

1 cup sugar

1 strip lemon peel

1 (2-inch) stick cinnamon

CHOCOLATE SABAYON

4 ounces semisweet chocolate

3/4 cup coffee, divided

9 egg yolks

5 tablespoons sugar

2 tablespoons pear brandy
or cognac

WHIPPED CREAM

1 cup whipping cream

2 tablespoons confectioners'
sugar

2 tablespoons pear brandy
or cognac

SERVES 6

Peel whole pears leaving stem intact. In a saucepan that will hold pears, combine water, sugar, peel, and cinnamon. Heat to boiling; add pears. Cover and poach until tender. Let pears cool in the syrup; refrigerate overnight.

*For the chocolate sabayon*: Melt chocolate in 1/4 cup hot coffee. In a double boiler, mix yolks and sugar. Add the melted chocolate and remaining coffee. Stir mixture over simmering water until creamy and thickened. Add brandy.

*For the whipped cream*: Whip cream; add in sugar and brandy.

To serve, place pears upright in a crystal dish. Pour chocolate sabayon sauce over pears and garnish with whipped cream.

# Chocolate-Dipped, Red Wine–Poached Pears with Crème Anglaise

PEARS

4 pears

4 cups water

1 cup red wine

1/2 cup sugar

1 tablespoon cinnamon

1 teaspoon cardamom

GANACHE

1 cup heavy cream

8 ounces dark chocolate

CRÈME ANGLAISE

2 cups cream, divided

1/2 cup sugar, divided

4 eggs

1 vanilla bean

SERVES 4

*For the pears*: Peel and core pears. Cut in half (try to keep stems) and place in shallow roasting pan. Cover with water. Add the wine, sugar, cinnamon, and cardamom. Bring to a boil on top of the stove, then cover with foil and cook in a 350 degree F oven until fork tender.

*For the ganache*: Bring the cream to a boil in a saucepan and add chocolate. Stir until melted, then remove from heat.

*For the crème anglaise*: Combine 1 cup cream and 1/4 cup sugar in a saucepan; bring to a boil. In a bowl, combine remaining cream and sugar; whisk in eggs and vanilla bean. Gradually add hot cream from saucepan into the cold liquid in the bowl. Return to heat and stir constantly until temperature reaches 165 degrees F. Cover and refrigerate.

Cool and dry pears thoroughly. Use a fork to dip pears into chocolate ganache and return to refrigerator for chocolate to set.

To serve, pool crème anglaise on a plate; swirl chocolate sauce to make design in the crème anglaise. Place pear in the center of the pool.

—*Andy Barnes, Executive Chef, Dinner For Two*

# Grilled Bananas with Ice Cream and Bourbon Caramel Sauce

BOURBON CARAMEL SAUCE

3 cups firmly packed dark brown sugar

3 cups heavy whipping cream

6 tablespoons unsalted butter

3 tablespoons honey

3 vanilla beans, halved lengthwise

3 tablespoons bourbon

BANANAS

10 large bananas, unpeeled

2 quarts vanilla ice cream

Chopped toasted pecans

SERVES 20

*For the caramel sauce*: Combine sugar, cream, butter, and honey in a heavy large saucepan. Scrape in vanilla seeds; add vanilla beans. Stir mixture over medium heat until sugar dissolves. Increase heat and bring to a boil. Reduce heat to medium-low and boil gently until sauce coats spoon thickly and is reduced to 3-2/3 cups, stirring occasionally, about 25 minutes. Mix in bourbon.

*For the bananas*: Heat barbecue to medium-high heat. Cut unpeeled bananas in half lengthwise. Place bananas, cut side up, on grill rack. Close barbecue; grill until peels are slightly charred and fruit is tender and beginning to come away from the peel, about 4 minutes.

To serve, place 1 grilled banana half, cut side up, on each plate. Top each with ice cream, warm caramel sauce, and pecans.

# Mangoes Drizzled with Spiced Honey

4 just-ripe mangoes

SPICED HONEY

1/2 cup fresh orange juice

1/4 cup fresh lime juice

2 tablespoons honey

1 teaspoon kosher salt

1 teaspoon pure chili powder

1 lime, cut into wedges

8 fresh mint sprigs

SERVES 4

To prepare each mango, stand it on end, stem end up, with the narrow side facing you. Slice straight down about 3/4 of an inch away from either side of the stem. Place the mango, cut side up, on a cutting board, and score the flesh with the tip of a sharp paring knife, making a diagonal 1/2-inch grid. Be certain to cut through the flesh deeply, but not through the skin. Repeat with remaining mango halves. Press against the skin side of each half mango so the mango flesh pops upward, creating a porcupine pattern. Repeat with the remaining mango halves. Set aside.

*For the spiced honey*: In a mixing bowl, whisk together the juices, honey, salt, and chili powder.

When ready to serve, place two mango halves overlapping on individual plates. Drizzle mangoes with the Spiced Honey. Garnish with the lime wedges and mint sprigs.

—*Emily Swanter, Las Cosas Cooking Class*

# Tarts and Pies

## Pink Adobe Legendary French Apple Pie

### CRUST
2 cups flour

3/4 cup lard

1 teaspoon salt

6 to 7 tablespoons cold water

### FILLING
1 (16-ounce) can apples, drained

2 tablespoons fresh lemon juice

1/2 teaspoon ground nutmeg

1/2 teaspoon ground cinnamon

1/2 cup sugar

1/4 cup seedless raisins

1 cup brown sugar

2 tablespoons flour

2 tablespoons butter

1/2 cup shelled pecans

1/2 cup milk

### RUM HARD SAUCE
1/2 cup butter

1-1/2 cups confectioners' sugar

1 tablespoon boiling water

1 teaspoon brandy or rum

SERVES 8

*For the crust*: Preheat oven to 450 degrees F. Work the flour, lard, and salt together with your fingers until crumbly. Add water until dough holds together. Divide into 2 equal balls. On a floured surface, roll out 1 ball thin enough to line a 9-inch pie pan. Roll out second ball in the same manner for the top crust.

*For the filling*: Place apples in pastry-lined pie pan and sprinkle with lemon juice, nutmeg, and cinnamon. Spread sugar and raisins evenly over apples. Mix brown sugar, flour, and butter in a bowl until well blended; spread over filling and sprinkle with pecans. Add most of the milk and cover with the top crust. Prick top with a fork and brush the remaining milk on the pastry. Bake for 10 minutes, then reduce heat to 350 degrees F and bake another 30 minutes. Crust should be golden brown when done.

*For the sauce*: Cream butter until light. Beat in sugar and add water. Beat in liquor and serve on each slice of pie.

—*Rosalea Murphy, The Pink Adobe*

Robert Henri (1865–1929), *Maria (Lucinda in Wrap)*, 1917. Oil on canvas, 24 x 20 in., Collection of the New Mexico Museum of Art. Bequest of Helen Miller Jones. Photograph by Blair Clark.

# Bavarian Apple Tart

**TART CRUST**

1/2 cup softened butter

1/3 cup sugar

1/4 teaspoon vanilla

1 cup flour

**FILLING**

1 (8-ounce) package cream
cheese, softened

1/4 cup sugar

1 egg

1/2 teaspoon vanilla

**TOPPING**

4 cups peeled apple slices

1/2 teaspoon cinnamon

1/3 cup sugar

1/4 cup sliced almonds

SERVES 8 TO 10

*For the crust*: Preheat oven to 450 degrees F. Combine all crust ingredients; do not overwork dough. Press dough into the bottom and halfway up the sides of an ungreased 9-inch springform pan.

*For the filling*: Blend all filling ingredients in a medium bowl. Pour over crust.

*For the topping*: Toss apples in cinnamon and sugar in a large bowl and arrange in layers over cheese mixture. Sprinkle top with almonds. Bake 10 minutes at 450 degrees F; reduce heat to 400 degrees F and bake 25 minutes more. Serve warm or chilled garnished with whipped cream, if desired.

*Tangy apples, such as McIntosh, Jonathan, Northern Spy, perhaps mixed with Granny Smith, are recommended.*

# Piñon Crumb Apple Pie

**CRUST**

1-1/2 cups flour

1/2 cup unsalted butter

3 tablespoons cold water

**FILLING**

6 cups apples, peeled and sliced

2 teaspoons vanilla

1/2 cup sugar

2 teaspoons cinnamon

2 tablespoons flour

**STREUSEL TOPPING**

1/2 cup unsalted butter

1/2 cup flour

2 teaspoons ground cinnamon

1 1/4 cups sugar

1 cup piñons

SERVES 6 TO 8

*For the crust*: Preheat oven to 350 degrees F. Make crust by placing flour in a medium-size bowl. Slice butter with a knife and add to bowl. Using a pastry blender, cut the butter until it is like oatmeal. Add the water and, using your fingertips, lightly mix and gather together into a ball. Remove the ball of dough to a floured work surface and, using just 3 to 5 strokes, knead it into a ball. Flatten the dough, wrap in plastic wrap and chill for 10 minutes. Roll the dough and place into an 8-inch pie pan.

*For the filling*: In a large bowl, toss together the filling ingredients and turn out into the pie crust.

*For the streusel topping*: Make the streusel by mixing the butter, flour, cinnamon, and sugar. Blend together until crumbly. Add the piñons and mix. Sprinkle on top of the apples. Bake for 45 minutes, or until the streusel is golden and the apples are soft and bubbly.

Chicago Slide Co., *Navajo camp fire*, ca. 1910–1920. Collection of the Palace of the Governors Photo Archives.

# Strawberry-Almond Cream Tart

SERVES 10

CRUST

36 honey graham crackers (about 9 sheets)

2 tablespoons sugar

2 tablespoons butter, melted

4 teaspoons water

FILLING

2/3 cup light cream cheese

1/4 cup sugar

1/2 teaspoon vanilla extract

1/4 teaspoon almond extract

TOPPING

6 cups small fresh strawberries, stemmed and hulled, divided

2/3 cup sugar

1 tablespoon cornstarch

1 tablespoon fresh lemon juice

2 tablespoons sliced almonds, toasted

*For the crust*: Preheat oven to 350 degrees F. Process graham crackers in a food processor until crumbly. Add sugar, butter, and water; pulse just until moist. Place mixture in a 9-inch round removable-bottom tart pan coated with cooking spray, pressing into the bottom and 3/4 inch up the sides of the pan. Bake for 10 minutes, or until lightly browned. Cool completely on a wire rack.

*For the filling*: Combine cream cheese, sugar, and extracts in a medium bowl; stir until smooth and well blended. Spread mixture evenly over the bottom of the tart shell.

*For the topping*: Place 2 cups strawberries in a food processor; process until puréed. Combine strawberry purée, sugar, and cornstarch in a small saucepan over medium heat, stirring with a whisk. Bring to a boil, stirring constantly. Reduce heat to low; cook 1 minute. Remove glaze from heat and cool to room temperature, stirring occasionally.

Combine remaining strawberries and lemon juice, toss to coat. Arrange berries, bottoms up, in a circular pattern over filling. Spoon half of glaze evenly over berries (reserve remaining glaze for another use). Sprinkle nuts around edge. Cover and chill 3 hours.

*This recipe works well with a 9-inch springform pan or a 10-inch pie pan or an 8 x 12-inch rectangular pan. To make tart up to 2 days ahead, prepare the crust and filling and refrigerate. Assemble with strawberry topping before serving.*

Gustave Baumann (1881–1971), *Talpa Chapel*, 1918–1922. Color woodcut, 5-3/4 x 7-1/2 in. Collection of New Mexico Museum of Art. Purchased with funds raised by School of American Research, 1952. Photograph by Blair Clark.

# Strawberry-Rhubarb Pie

Pastry for a 2-crust pie

FILLING

2 cups fresh rhubarb cut into 1-inch pieces or 1 pound bag frozen rhubarb, thawed and drained

2 cups halved fresh strawberries, hulled

2 to 3 tablespoons lemon juice, to taste

1-1/4 cups plus 1 tablespoon sugar, divided

1/8 teaspoon salt

1/3 cup flour

2 tablespoons unsalted butter

1 egg beaten with 1 tablespoon water

SERVES 6 TO 8

Preheat oven 350 degrees F. Roll out half of pastry dough into a 1/8-inch-thick circle and place it in a 9-inch pie pan. Reserve remaining pastry for lattice top; wrap and chill in refrigerator. Line dough with foil and fill with beans or pie weights and bake for 20 minutes, until light brown. Cool slightly.

*For the filling*: Toss the rhubarb, strawberries, and lemon juice together in a large bowl. Spoon half of the fruit filling into the pie shell. Combine 1-1/4 cups sugar, salt, and flour; sprinkle half over the fruit filling. Spread remaining fruit filling over sugar mixture and sprinkle overall with remaining sugar mixture; dot top with butter.

Preheat oven 450 degrees F. Roll remaining pastry dough into a circle. Cut dough into strips; weave into crisscross pattern atop filling to form lattice-top crust. Brush egg wash over strips and sprinkle with 1 tablespoon sugar overall. Bake pie for 10 minutes, then reduce oven temperature to 350 degrees F and bake for 40 minutes, until rhubarb is tender and crust is brown. Remove from oven and cool on a rack.

# Strawberry-Chocolate Tart

SERVES 8

## CRUST

10 ounces finely chopped almonds

1 cup unsalted butter, at room temperature

1/3 cup sugar

3 cups flour

1 egg, beaten

1 teaspoon vanilla or almond extract

## FILLING

1 cup semisweet chocolate pieces

2 tablespoons butter, melted

3 tablespoons Kirsch liqueur

1/4 cup confectioners' sugar, sifted

1 tablespoon water

## TOPPING

1-1/2 pints strawberries, washed, stemmed, and dried

3 tablespoons currant jelly

1 tablespoon Kirsch liqueur

Mint sprigs, for garnish

*For the crust*: Mix together all ingredients until well blended. Divide mixture in half and press into two (9-inch) buttered springform tart pans or twelve (3-inch) tartlet pans. Chill for 30 minutes. Meanwhile, preheat oven to 350 degrees F. Bake crusts for 15 to 20 minutes until golden brown. Cool.

*For the filling*: Melt chocolate in a bowl over simmering water in a saucepan. When chocolate has reached 110 degrees F, add melted butter and Kirsch. Whisk until smooth. Add confectioners' sugar and water, continuing to whisk until smooth. While mixture is warm, pour into tart shells.

*For the topping*: Place strawberries tips up in a circular pattern over warm chocolate filling. In a small saucepan, whisk currant jelly and Kirsch over medium heat until smooth. Spoon warm glaze over strawberries. Refrigerate finished tarts for 2 hours. Remove from refrigerator 45 minutes before serving. Garnish with mint sprigs.

# Strawberry and White Chocolate Mousse Tart

1-1/4 cups unbleached flour

1/4 cup sugar

1/4 teaspoon salt

1/2 cup chilled unsalted butter, cut into 1/2-inch pieces

1 large egg yolk

1 tablespoon (or more) ice water

MOUSSE

6 ounces good-quality white chocolate, chopped

1-1/4 cups chilled whipping cream, divided

1/2 teaspoon vanilla extract

2 large egg whites

1/8 teaspoon cream of tartar

TOPPING

1/3 cup seedless strawberry jam

1 tablespoon fresh lemon juice

1 (16-ounce) basket strawberries, hulled, thinly sliced lengthwise

SERVES 8

*For the crust*: Blend flour, sugar, and salt in a food processor. Cut in butter by pulsing until mixture resembles coarse meal. Whisk egg yolk and 1 tablespoon ice water in small bowl to blend; add to processor and process until moist clumps form, adding more ice water by teaspoons if dough is dry. Gather dough into ball; flatten into disk shape. Roll out dough on a floured surface to a 13-inch circle. Transfer dough to a 9-inch diameter tart pan with removable bottom. Trim overhang to 1/2 inch. Fold overhang in and press onto sides, forming double-thick sides. Pierce crust bottom all over with a fork; freeze for 30 minutes.

Preheat oven to 375 degrees F. Line crust with foil; fill with dried beans or pie weights. Bake until crust sides are light brown, about 25 minutes. Remove foil and beans; bake until crust is golden brown, about 20 minutes longer. Cool crust completely in pan on a rack.

*For the mousse*: Combine white chocolate and 1/4 cup whipping cream in large metal bowl. Set bowl over a saucepan of simmering water (do not allow bottom of bowl to touch water) and stir until chocolate is melted and smooth. Remove bowl from over water; cool chocolate mixture until lukewarm, about 15 minutes.

Beat remaining whipping cream and vanilla in large bowl until peaks form. Using clean dry beaters, beat egg whites with cream of tartar in a medium bowl until stiff but not dry. Fold whites into chocolate mixture, then fold in whipped cream. Transfer mixture to the cooled crust; smooth top. Chill overnight.

*For the topping*: Combine jam and lemon juice in small saucepan; bring to simmer, stirring over medium heat until jam melts. Remove from heat. Arrange strawberries in concentric circles atop tart. Brush berries with melted jam mixture. Chill tart up to 2 hours and serve.

# Grandma Lucy's Strawberry Pie

PASTRY SHELL

1-1/2 cups flour

1/2 cup unsalted butter, cut into pieces

1/4 cup ice water

FILLING

6 cups firm ripe strawberries, divided

1/2 cup water

3 tablespoons cornstarch

1 tablespoon fresh lemon juice

1-1/4 cups sugar

1/4 teaspoon salt

TOPPING

1/2 cup heavy cream, whipped

1 tablespoon sugar

1/4 teaspoon vanilla

SERVES 6 TO 8

*For the pastry shell*: Preheat oven to 350 degrees F. Using a food processor, combine flour and butter and pulse until the mixture looks like cornmeal. Gradually add up to 1/4 cup ice water until dough forms into a ball. Remove dough and flatten into a disk shape. Wrap in plastic wrap and refrigerate until chilled, about 30 minutes. Roll dough out on a floured surface, and then place in a 9-inch pie pan. Bake until light brown, about 20 minutes.

*For the filling*: Wash and hull strawberries. Mix half with water, cornstarch, lemon juice, sugar, and salt; crush.

In a medium saucepan, over medium-low heat, cook mixture, stirring constantly, until very thick; cool. Turn remaining berries into cooled pie crust. Cover with the cooled cooked filling. Chill in the refrigerator at least 3 hours.

*For the topping*: Sweeten whipped cream with sugar and add vanilla.

# Buttermilk Tart with Raspberries

Pastry for a 12-inch tart pan

FILLING

2-1/4 cups sugar

3 tablespoons flour

5 tablespoons unsalted butter, melted and cooled to room temperature

3 large eggs, lightly beaten

1-1/2 cups buttermilk

1 teaspoon vanilla extract

1 teaspoon red wine vinegar

TOPPING

1 (16-ounce) jar apricot preserves

2 tablespoons bourbon

2 pints raspberries, rinsed and drained

SERVES 6 TO 8

Preheat oven to 375 degrees F. Roll out dough on floured surface and carefully place in 1 (12-inch) tart pan with removable bottom. Line the dough with foil and fill with beans or rice. Bake shell 25 to 30 minutes.

*For the filling*: Combine sugar and flour in a large mixing bowl. Add butter and mix well. Place eggs in a medium bowl and gently whisk in buttermilk, vanilla, and vinegar. Stir the egg mixture into the flour mixture, again mixing gently so as not to incorporate any air. Pour the filling into the crust and bake for 20 to 30 minutes, until filling is lightly set in the middle or until a tester inserted in the center comes out clean. Place on a rack to cool for 10 minutes. Remove sides of pan and let cool to room temperature. Refrigerate until completely set, at least 1-1/2 hours. Tart can be made a day ahead up to this point.

*For the topping*: Make glaze by heating preserves and bourbon in a heavy pan until melted. Press mixture through a sieve and remove any bits of fruit from the glaze. Arrange raspberries decoratively on top of the tart and brush tops and sides of crust with warm glaze. Let stand at least 30 minutes at room temperature before serving.

# Frozen Grand Marnier and Chocolate Cranberry Torte

## CRUST

1 (9-ounce) package chocolate wafer cookies

1/2 cup semisweet chocolate chips

3 tablespoons sugar

7 tablespoons unsalted butter, melted

## FILLING

8 large egg yolks

1 cup sugar

1/4 cup water

1/2 teaspoon ground nutmeg

1/8 teaspoon ground allspice

2 cups chilled heavy whipping cream

1/2 cup chilled sour cream

5 tablespoons Grand Marnier or other orange liqueur

3 tablespoons frozen orange juice concentrate, thawed

1 tablespoon grated orange zest

## TOPPING

1/2 cup ruby port

1 tablespoon cornstarch

1 cup sugar

1/4 cup honey

1 teaspoon ground nutmeg

1 teaspoon ground allspice

1/2 teaspoon ground cinnamon

5 cups fresh cranberries, divided

White chocolate curls for garnish

SERVES 12

*For the crust*: Finely grind cookies, chocolate chips, and sugar in a processor. Add melted butter; blend until wet crumbs form. Set aside 1/2 cup crumb mixture. Press remaining crumb mixture onto the bottom and 2 inches up the sides of a 9-inch diameter springform pan with 2-3/4-inch-high sides.

*For the filling*: Whisk the first 3 ingredients in a medium metal bowl. Set over a saucepan of simmering water and whisk vigorously until a candy thermometer registers 175 degrees F, about 8 minutes. Remove bowl from heat. Add spices. Using mixer, beat until thick and cool, about 5 minutes.

Using an electric mixer, beat whipping cream, sour cream, liqueur, juice concentrate, and zest in a large bowl until peaks form. Add egg yolk mixture and fold together. Pour two-thirds of filling into crust. Sprinkle with reserved 1/2 cup crumb mixture. Gently spoon remaining filling over. Cover; freeze overnight or up to 3 days.

*For the topping*: Whisk port and cornstarch in a large skillet to blend. Add sugar, honey, and spices. Bring mixture to boil over high heat, stirring often. Add 3 cups cranberries; cook until mixture boils and cranberries begin to pop but still hold their shape, about 5 minutes. Mix in remaining 2 cups cranberries. Chill topping mixture at least 6 hours or overnight. To serve, release pan sides from torte; transfer to a platter. Spoon topping over filling. Garnish torte with chocolate curls.

Anonymous artist, *Toy Horse*, c. 1960. India. Painted wood, 10 in high. Alexander Girard Foundation Collection. Museum of International Folk Art. Photograph by Michael Monteaux. A.1981.22.658.

# Fresh Peach Pie

NO-ROLL PIECRUST

1-1/2 cups flour

2 teaspoons sugar

1/2 teaspoon salt

1/2 cup vegetable oil

2 tablespoons milk

FILLING

1-1/2 cups sugar

4 tablespoons flour

1 teaspoon cinnamon

1 cup heavy whipping cream

6 good-size ripe peaches, peeled and sliced

SERVES 6 TO 8

*For the crust*: Preheat oven to 425 degrees F. Mix flour, sugar, and salt in a bowl, then transfer to a 9-inch pie pan. Add oil and milk. Mix ingredients well in pie pan, then carefully press dough into place and finish pie shell with fluted edges. Bake for 8 minutes. Remove pie crust from oven and cool.

*For the filling*: Reduce oven temperature to 400 degrees F. Combine sugar, flour, cinnamon, and cream; blend well. Add peaches. Pour filling into pie crust and bake for 15 minutes. Reduce temperature again to 350 degrees F and bake pie for an additional 45 minutes. Remove from oven and allow pie to cool. Refrigerate for at least 8 hours before serving. To serve, allow to come to room temperature.

*Colorado peaches recommended.*

Chicago Transparency Co., *Museum of Fine Arts viewed from the Plaza, Santa Fe*, ca. 1920. Collection of the Palace of the Governors Photo Archives.

# Fresh Apricot or Peach Tart

8 to 10 fresh apricots or 3 to 4
    freestone peaches

2/3 cup sugar, divided

1 (8-inch) tart shell, partially baked

2 tablespoons butter cut into
    pea-size dots

GLAZE

1/2 cup apricot preserves forced
    through a sieve

2 tablespoons sugar

1/4 cup slivered almonds

SERVES  8

Preheat oven to 375 degrees F. In a large saucepan, drop fruit into boiling water for 10 to 15 seconds. Peel, halve, and remove pits. Slice fruit if you wish, or cut into halves. Sprinkle 3 tablespoons sugar in the bottom of tart shell. Arrange fruit slices over the sugar in a closely overlapping layer of concentric circles. If fruit is halved, place the halves, domed side up, closely together in the shell. Sprinkle remaining sugar over fruit. Dot top of tart with the butter. Bake in the middle of the oven for 30 to 40 minutes, or until fruit is lightly colored and juices have become syrupy. Remove tart from the oven and place on a rack.

*For the glaze:* Stir the strained apricot preserves with sugar over medium heat for 2 to 3 minutes until thick enough to coat a spoon with a light film. Do not allow to boil.

Decorate tart with slivered almonds and spread warm glaze over top. Serve warm or cold.

# Apricot Empanadas

PASTRY

2 cups sifted flour

1 teaspoon baking powder

1/2 teaspoon salt

1/8 teaspoon ground coriander seed

1/2 cup shortening

1/3 cup (or more) cold milk

1 egg beaten with 1 tablespoon water

Sugar to sprinkle

FILLING

1/2 pound dried apricots

1/4 cup orange juice or water

1-1/4 cups sugar, or to taste

1/4 teaspoon salt

1 teaspoon ground cinnamon

1/2 teaspoon ground nutmeg

1/2 cup raisins, soaked in warm water or peach brandy, drained

SERVES 14

*For the pastry:* Mix flour, baking powder, salt, and coriander seed. Cut in shortening with a pastry blender or with fingers until the mixture becomes like coarse meal. Add milk, a few drops at a time, mixing dough until it comes together and forms a ball. Flatten dough into a disk shape, wrap in plastic wrap, and refrigerate 30 minutes.

*For the filling:* In a medium saucepan, simmer apricots in hot water or orange juice to cover until soft, about 20 minutes. Drain and cool. Mash fruit with hand-held masher or fork. Add remaining ingredients and mix well.

*To finish:* Preheat oven to 450 degrees F. Roll out dough to a thin sheet on a floured work surface; with cookie cutter, cut out 4-inch circles. Place a teaspoonful of fruit filling on the center of each circle. Brush edges of circle with egg wash and fold in half. Carefully press the edges together to seal them well with fork tines. Place empanadas on a baking sheet lightly coated with cooking spray; brush the tops lightly with egg wash and sprinkle with sugar. Bake until golden brown, about 15 minutes. Remove empanadas from the oven and allow to cool on wire racks.

# Kiwi Tart

1 (9-inch) round of refrigerated pie dough

FILLING

6 ounces cream cheese, softened slightly

2 tablespoons sugar

2 tablespoons milk

1 teaspoon finely grated fresh lemon zest

1/2 teaspoon vanilla

3 firm-ripe kiwis, peeled and thinly sliced

SERVES 8

Preheat oven to 450 degrees F with the rack in middle position. Fit dough into an 8-3/4- to 9-1/4-inch deep tart pan with a removable bottom. Leave a 1/2-inch overhang; then fold overhang inward and press against side of pan to reinforce the edge. Lightly prick the bottom and sides of shell with a fork. Line tart shell with foil and fill with pie weights. Bake until the edge is pale golden, about 10 minutes. Carefully remove foil and weights and bake shell until golden all over, an additional 5 minutes. Cool shell in the pan on a rack, about 20 minutes.

*For the filling:* Beat together cream cheese, sugar, milk, zest, and vanilla in a bowl with an electric mixer until creamy and smooth, 2 to 3 minutes. Spread cream cheese filling into cooled shell and top with kiwi slices. Tart can be made 4 hours ahead and chilled, covered. Bring to room temperature before serving.

# Honey-Caramel Tart
## with Apricots and Almonds

SERVES 10 TO 12

### CRUST

1 1/2 cups all-purpose flour

1/2 cup semolina flour (pasta flour)*

1/4 teaspoon salt

1/2 cup unsalted butter, at room temperature

1/3 cup firmly packed golden brown sugar

2 tablespoons honey

1 teaspoon lemon zest

1 large egg

### FILLING

3/4 cup firmly packed light brown sugar

1/4 cup sugar

1/4 cup unsalted butter

1/4 cup honey

1/2 cup dried cherries

1/2 cup coarsely chopped dried apricots

1/2 cup whole almonds, toasted, coarsely chopped

1/4 cup dried cranberries

1-1/4 cups chilled whipping cream, divided

1 (15-ounce) can apricot halves, drained, patted dry

1 cup crème fraîche or sour cream

*For the crust*: Preheat oven to 350 degrees F. Whisk flours and salt in a medium bowl. Using an electric mixer, beat butter, brown sugar, honey, and zest in another medium bowl to blend. Beat in egg. Add flour mixture; beat just to blend. Gather dough into a ball. Roll out on a floured surface to a 1/4-inch-thick circle. Place pastry in a 9-inch tart pan with a removable bottom. Press dough onto the bottom and up the sides of the pan without stretching it. Trim edges and press so sides rise 1/4 inch above the pan. Bake crust until golden brown, about 13 minutes. If bubbles form while baking, press with the back of a fork. Cool on a rack.

*For the filling*: Bring sugars, butter, and honey to a boil in a heavy medium saucepan, stirring to dissolve sugars. Boil 1 minute without stirring; remove from heat. Stir in cherries, dried apricots, almonds, cranberries, and 1/4 cup cream. Pour filling into the cooled crust. Arrange apricot halves, cut side down, atop filling. Bake tart at 350 degrees F until bubbly, about 1 hour and 20 minutes; cool on a rack for 15 minutes. Remove pan sides. Cool 1 more hour until tart is lukewarm. Using an electric mixer, beat 1 cup cream until peaks form. Add crème fraîche and beat to blend. Top filling with crème mixture. Serve the tart slightly warm or at room temperature.

*Semolina flour is available at some supermarkets, Italian markets, or specialty foods stores.*

# Two-Layer Key Lime Pie

3/4 cup granola (without raisins or other dried fruit)

3/4 cup graham cracker crumbs (about 6 graham cracker sheets)

1/4 cup unsalted butter, melted

3 tablespoons sugar

BAKED LAYER

1 (14-ounce) can sweetened condensed milk

1/2 cup fresh Key lime juice or lime juice

3 large egg yolks

CHILLED LAYER

1 (8-ounce) package cream cheese, at room temperature

1/2 cup sweetened condensed milk

1/4 cup fresh Key lime juice or lime juice

2 tablespoons sugar

1 teaspoon vanilla

Whipped cream for garnish

SERVES 8

*For the crust*: Preheat oven to 350 degrees F. Blend granola in a food processor, pulsing, until coarsely ground. Transfer granola to a medium bowl. Mix in graham cracker crumbs, butter, and sugar. Press crumb mixture over the bottom and up the sides of a 9-inch-diameter deep-dish glass pie dish. Bake until crust is golden brown, about 8 minutes. Reduce oven temperature to 300 degrees F. Remove crust from oven and cool completely.

*For the baked layer*: Whisk condensed milk, lime juice, and egg yolks in a medium bowl to blend. Pour into pie crust. Bake until custard is set, about 25 minutes.

*For the chilled layer*: Using an electric mixer, beat cream cheese, condensed milk, lime juice, sugar, and vanilla in a large bowl. Pour over cooled baked layer; smooth the top. Cover and chill until firm, at least 4 hours. Garnish with whipped cream.

# White Chocolate and Lime Tart

GRAHAM CRACKER CRUST

8 ounces graham crackers

1/4 cup sugar

6 tablespoons melted butter

4 ounces bittersweet chocolate, melted

FILLING

3/4 cup heavy cream

1/2 cup milk

12 ounces white chocolate, chopped

Grated zest of 2 limes, plus julienned zest of 1 lime

Juice from 3 limes

Bittersweet and white chocolate shavings for garnish

SERVES 10

*For the crust*: Preheat oven to 350 degrees F. Coat a 10-inch tart pan with butter. Process the crackers and sugar in a food processor until fine crumbs form. Add the butter and blend well. Press crumb mixture evenly over the bottom and up the sides of the pan. Bake about 7 to 9 minutes, or until golden brown.

Pour melted chocolate into the crust and, using a rubber spatula, spread evenly to cover the bottom and sides of the crust. Let crust cool to harden the chocolate before filling.

*For the filling*: Heat cream and milk to just below simmering. Add chocolate and grated zest. Stir until all chocolate is melted, and add lime juice. Set aside to cool. Pour filling into prepared chocolate-lined crust and spread evenly. Refrigerate until firm. Garnish with julienned zest and both white and dark chocolate shavings.

# Lemon Crème Brulée Tart

**CRUST**

1 cup flour

1/4 cup confectioners' sugar

Pinch of salt

6 tablespoons chilled unsalted butter, cut into 1/2-inch cubes

4 teaspoons (or more) chilled whipping cream

1 egg white, beaten to blend

**FILLING**

3/4 cup plus 2 tablespoons sugar, divided

3/4 cup whipping cream

4 large egg yolks

2 large eggs

1/2 cup fresh lemon juice

1 tablespoon packed finely grated lemon zest

Lemon slices for garnish

**SERVES 8**

*For the crust*: Combine flour, sugar, and salt in a processor; blend 5 seconds. Pulsing, blend in butter until coarse meal forms. Add 4 teaspoons cream. Pulse until moist clumps form, adding more cream by teaspoons if dough is dry. Remove dough and gather into a ball; flatten into disk shape. Wrap in plastic wrap and chill at least 2 hours.

Preheat oven to 350 degrees F. Roll out dough on floured surface to a 12-inch round; transfer to a 9-inch diameter tart pan with a removable bottom. Fold overhang in, pressing to form double-thick edges. Bake shell until golden, pressing with back of fork if crust bubbles, about 18 minutes (small cracks may appear). Brush inside of hot crust twice with egg white. Maintain oven temperature.

*For the filling*: Whisk 3/4 cup sugar, cream, yolks, and eggs in a bowl to blend well. Mix in lemon juice and zest. Pour filling into the warm crust. Bake until filling is slightly puffed at the edges and set in the center, about 30 minutes. Cool completely, about 1 hour.

Preheat broiler. Place tart on a baking sheet and cover edge of crust with foil to prevent burning.

Sprinkle tart with 2 tablespoons sugar. Broil tart until sugar melts and caramelizes, turning sheet for even browning, about 2 minutes. Transfer tart to a rack. Cool until topping is crisp, about 1 hour. Push bottom of tart pan up, releasing the tart; place on a platter. Garnish tart with lemon slices.

# Blueberry Lemon Cream Tarts

**CRUST**

1 cup graham cracker crumbs

1-1/2 tablespoons sugar

4 tablespoons unsalted butter, melted

**FILLING**

2 tablespoons firmly packed light brown sugar

1/4 cup sour cream

1/4 teaspoon vanilla

4 ounces cream cheese, softened

1/2 teaspoon finely grated fresh lemon zest

**TOPPING**

1-1/3 cups (6 ounces) blueberries

Confectioners' sugar for dusting

**SERVES 4**

*For the crust*: Preheat oven to 350 degrees F with a baking sheet on the middle rack. Stir together graham cracker crumbs, sugar, and butter in a bowl until well combined, then press mixture with your fingers and the back of a spoon evenly and firmly onto the bottom and up the sides of four (3-3/4-inch) nonstick fluted tart pans or four (8-ounce) ramekins. (If using ramekins, press mixture 3/4 inch up sides.)

Place tart pans on the preheated baking sheet and bake crusts until slightly darker, about 10 minutes, then cool 10 minutes on a rack. (Ramekins need to cool 5 minutes in the refrigerator.) Gently push on the bottom of each tart pan to loosen crust; then invert crust onto your hand and place on a serving plate. (If using ramekins, leave crusts in ramekins.)

*For the filling*: While crusts cool, whisk together brown sugar, sour cream, and vanilla in a small bowl until sugar is dissolved. Beat cream cheese in a medium bowl with an electric mixer until smooth; then add sour cream mixture and zest, beating until just combined well. Divide cream cheese filling among tart shells, spreading evenly. Store tarts in refrigerator before serving. To serve, top tarts with blueberries and dust with confectioners' sugar.

Probably from Panduro Family Workshop, *Figure: Elf with Fruit*, c. 1970. San Pedro Tlaque-paque, Jalisco, Mexico. Painted earthenware, 2-7/8 in high. Girard Foundation Collection. Museum of International Folk Art. Photograph by Michael Monteaux. A.1979.5.669x.

# Honey Pecan Pie

1/2 cup butter

1 cup sugar

3 eggs, beaten

1/2 cup corn syrup

1/2 cup honey

1/2 teaspoon fresh lemon juice

1 teaspoon vanilla

1 cup chopped pecans

Pinch of cinnamon

Pinch of nutmeg

1 (9-inch) unbaked pie crust

SERVES 8 TO 10

Preheat oven to 425 degrees F. In a heavy sauté pan, brown butter to a caramel color over medium heat. Remove and allow butter to cool slightly. In a large mixing bowl, combine sugar, eggs, syrup, and honey. Using a wire whisk, blend well. Add the browned butter, lemon juice, vanilla, and pecans. Add cinnamon and nutmeg. Pour into pie crust and bake on the center rack of oven for 10 minutes; then reduce temperature to 375 degrees F and bake for 35 minutes. Remove from oven and allow to cool.

# Two Pecan Chiffon Pies

1 cup coarsely chopped pecans

1 cup dark brown sugar

1-1/3 cups plus 2 tablespoons water

4 tablespoons cornstarch

1/4 cup water

2/3 cup egg whites (about 2 large eggs), at room temperature

1/4 cup sugar

2 (8-inch) pie shells, baked

1/2 pint whipping cream

SERVES 16

Preheat oven to 250 degrees F. Spread pecans on a baking sheet and bake for 10 to 15 minutes, or until nuts barely begin to brown. Take care not to burn. Reserve 2 tablespoons pecans for garnish. In a saucepan, combine brown sugar and 1-1/3 cups plus 2 tablespoons water. Bring to a boil. Mix together cornstarch and 1/4 cup water and stir with a whisk into the boiling brown sugar mixture. Stir constantly and cook until mixture becomes clear and is the consistency of thick pudding. Remove the mixture from heat.

Whip egg whites at high speed in a mixer until peaks form. Slowly add sugar and beat until peaks are stiff. Reduce mixer speed to low and gently add hot brown sugar mixture and nuts. Mix until just blended (do not over mix). Lightly spoon filling into baked pie shells. To serve, whip cream until stiff, divide, and spread over both pies. Sprinkle with reserved toasted pecans on top. Refrigerate.

*Pies are best when served the same day. Use ultra-pasteurized eggs as eggs in this recipe are not thoroughly cooked.*

# Cinnamon Streusel Pumpkin Pie

1 (9-inch) frozen pie shell, thawed

FILLING

3/4 teaspoon ground cinnamon

1/4 teaspoon ground allspice

1/4 teaspoon ground ginger

1/4 teaspoon ground nutmeg

1/8 teaspoon ground cloves

2 large eggs

1 (15-ounce) can unsweetened pumpkin

1 (14-ounce) can sweetened condensed milk

STREUSEL

1/3 cup flour

1/3 cup firmly packed dark brown sugar

1/4 cup regular oats

1/4 cup chopped pecans

3/4 teaspoon ground cinnamon

1/8 teaspoon ground ginger

2 tablespoons chilled butter, cut into small pieces

2 to 3 teaspoons water

SERVES 10 TO 12

Preheat oven to 375 degrees F. Roll dough to an 11-inch circle. Transfer to a 9-inch pie plate coated with cooking spray. Fold overhang under and flute edges.

*For the filling*: Combine all ingredients in a large bowl and stir well with a whisk. Pour pumpkin mixture into pastry shell.

*For the streusel*: Lightly spoon flour into measuring cup; level. Combine flour with next 5 ingredients in a bowl. Cut in butter with a fork or fingertips until crumbly. Sprinkle with water, tossing with a fork until lightly moistened. Sprinkle streusel over filled pie.

Place pie on a baking sheet and bake for 50 minutes, or until a tester inserted in the center comes out clean. Remove from baking sheet; cool completely on a wire rack.

# Chocolate Angel Pie

2 egg whites

1/8 teaspoon salt

1/8 teaspoon cream of tartar

1/2 cup sugar

1/2 teaspoon vanilla

1/2 cup nuts

FILLING

1 (4-ounce) bar German's Sweet
Chocolate

3 tablespoons water

1 teaspoon vanilla

8 ounces whipping cream,
whipped

Chocolate curls, for garnish

SERVES 6

*For the meringue crust*: Preheat oven to 350 degrees F. Beat egg whites with salt and cream of tartar until foamy. Add sugar, 2 tablespoons at a time, beating well after each addition; then continue to beat to very stiff peaks. Fold in vanilla and nuts. Spoon the meringue into a lightly greased 8-inch pie pan to form a nestlike shell; build sides up 1/2 inch above the edge of the pan. Bake 55 to 60 minutes.

*For the filling*: Stir chocolate in water over low heat until melted; cool until thickened. Add 1 teaspoon vanilla. Transfer to a bowl and fold whipped cream into chocolate mixture. Pile into meringue shell. Chill at least 2 hours. To serve, garnish with chocolate curls on top.

# Chocolate Pecan Pie

PIE CRUST

40 vanilla wafers

2 tablespoons brown sugar

1 tablespoon butter, melted

1 large egg white, lightly beaten

FILLING

1/2 cup coarsely chopped pecans,
toasted

1/3 cup semisweet chocolate
chips

2/3 cup dark corn syrup

1/2 cup firmly packed brown sugar

3 tablespoons bourbon

1 teaspoon vanilla extract

1/4 teaspoon salt

3 large eggs, lightly beaten

SERVES 10

*For the crust*: Preheat oven to 350 degrees F. Place wafers in a food processor; pulse until finely ground. Add brown sugar, butter, and egg white; pulse 2 to 3 times, or just until moistened. Press mixture into the bottom and up the sides of a 9-inch pie pan coated with cooking spray. Bake for 5 minutes. Cool on a wire rack.

*For the filling*: Sprinkle pecans and chocolate chips on the bottom of the prepared crust. Combine remaining ingredients, stirring well with a whisk. Pour over pecans and chocolate chips. Bake for 27 minutes, or until set. Cool on a wire rack.

Anonymous artist, *Plate*, c. 1960. Tonalá, Jalisco, Mexico. Glazed earthenware, 8-3/4 in diameter. Girard Foundation Collection. Museum of International Folk Art. Photograph by Michael Monteaux. A.1979.6.276x.

# Brandy Alexander Pie

1 envelope unflavored gelatin

1/2 cup cold water

2/3 cup sugar, divided

1/8 teaspoon salt

3 eggs, separated

1/4 cup cognac

1/4 cup Crème de Cacao or Kahlúa

2 cups heavy cream, whipped and divided

1 (9-inch) prebaked pie crust

Chocolate curls for garnish

SERVES 6 TO 8

Sprinkle gelatin over cold water in saucepan. Add 1/3 cup sugar, salt, and egg yolks. Stir to blend. Heat over low heat until gelatin dissolves and mixture thickens. Remove from heat; stir in cognac and liqueur. Chill until mixture mounds slightly, about 15 to 20 minutes. Meanwhile, beat egg whites until stiff and then gradually beat in remaining sugar. Fold gently into gelatin mixture and then fold in 1 cup of whipped cream. Turn into pie crust and chill overnight or for several hours.

To serve, top pie with remaining whipped cream and garnish with chocolate curls.

*Use ultra-pasteurized eggs as eggs in this recipe are not thoroughly cooked.*

# Date Chocolate Torte

1/2 pound unblanched almonds

1/2 pound semisweet chocolate

6 egg whites

1/2 cup sugar

1/2 pound dates, chopped finely

Whipped cream for garnish

Grated chocolate, nuts, or strawberries for garnish

SERVES 8 TO 10

Preheat oven to 350 degrees F. Place the almonds and chocolate in a blender or food processor and chop into chunky pieces. In a large bowl, beat the egg whites to stiff peaks and gradually add the sugar. Fold in the almonds, chocolate, and dates. Pour into a greased, foil-lined 9-inch springform pan and bake for 45 minutes. Open the oven door slightly and allow the torte to cool in the pan. When cool, turn onto a platter and refrigerate overnight. To serve, spread the top of the torte with whipped cream and decorate with grated chocolate, nuts, or strawberries.

*The torte will crumble if cut while still warm. It keeps in the refrigerator for several days.*

# Fig and Almond Tart

PIE CRUST

1/2 cup unsalted butter, melted and cooled

1/2 cup sugar

1/8 teaspoon almond extract

1/8 teaspoon vanilla extract

Pinch of salt

1-1/4 cups plus 1 tablespoon unbleached, all-purpose flour

2 tablespoons ground unblanched almonds

FILLING

1/2 cup heavy cream

1 large egg, lightly beaten

1/2 teaspoon almond extract

1/2 teaspoon vanilla extract

2 tablespoons raw full-flavored honey, like lavender

1 tablespoon superfine flour, like Wondra

1-1/2 pounds fresh figs, halved lengthwise (do not peel)

Confectioners' sugar

SERVES 8

*For the crust:* Preheat oven to 375 degrees F. Butter sides and bottom of a springform or 9-inch tart pan with a removable bottom and set aside. In a large bowl, combine melted butter and sugar and blend with a wooden spoon. Add extracts, salt, and flour and stir to form a soft, cookie-like dough. Do not let it form into a ball. Transfer the dough to the center of the tart pan. Using your fingers, press the dough evenly onto the bottom and sides. (It will be quite thin.) If using a springform pan, press the dough 1-1/2 inches up the side. Bake until the dough is slightly puffy and set, about 12 to 15 minutes. Remove from the oven and sprinkle almonds on the crust.

*For the filling:* In a medium bowl, combine the cream, egg, extracts, and honey and whisk to blend. Whisk in the flour. Starting just inside the edge of the tart shell, neatly overlap the figs, cut side up, at a slight angle. Make 2 or 3 concentric circles, working toward the center, and fill the center with the remaining figs.

Whisk the cream mixture again and pour evenly over the fruit. Place the tart in the center of the oven with a baking sheet on the rack below to catch any drips. Bake until the filling is firm and the pastry is a deep golden brown, about 50 or 60 minutes. Remove and sprinkle with confectioners' sugar just before serving.

*Unpeeled apricots or plums may be substituted for the figs.*

# Red-Gold Raspberry White Chocolate Tart

PIE CRUST

2 cups blanched almonds

1/4 cup sugar, divided

1/4 cup melted butter

1/2 cup seedless raspberry jam

FILLING

2/3 cup whipping cream

8 ounces white chocolate, chopped

2 tablespoons fresh lemon juice

1/2 teaspoon almond extract

2-1/4 cups red raspberries, rinsed and drained

2 cups golden raspberries, rinsed and drained (or use red raspberries)

1 tablespoon almond-flavor liqueur

SERVES 8

*For the crust*: Preheat oven to 325 degrees F. In a blender or food processor, process almonds with 2 tablespoons sugar until finely ground; if using a blender, whirl half of the mixture at a time. Pour nut mixture into a 9-inch tart pan with a removable bottom. Add butter and rub with fingers until mixture forms fine crumbs. Press nut mixture evenly over the bottom and up the side of the pan until flush with the rim. Bake crust until dark gold, about 20 minutes. Spread bottom of crust with jam. Cool on a rack.

*For the filling*: In a 1- to 2-quart saucepan over medium heat, stir cream and chocolate until smoothly melted, about 2 minutes. Stir in lemon juice and almond extract. Spoon evenly into the crust. Chill tart until filling is firm to touch, 1 to 1-1/4 hours.

Arrange red raspberries in a single layer on filling. In a blender or food processor, process golden raspberries, the remaining 2 tablespoons sugar, and liqueur until smoothly puréed. Press mixture through a fine strainer into a bowl; discard seeds. Evenly spread golden raspberry sauce in the center of dessert plates. Remove rim from tart pan. Cut tart into wedges and place a wedge in the sauce on each plate.

# White Balsamic Custard Tart with Fresh Berry Topping

CRUST

1-1/4 cups flour

3 tablespoons sugar

1/4 teaspoon salt

1/2 cup chilled unsalted butter, cut into 1/2-inch cubes

1 large egg yolk

1 tablespoon whipping cream

FILLING

1/2 cup whipping cream

2 tablespoons cornstarch

2 large eggs

4 large egg yolks

1 teaspoon vanilla

1/2 cup white balsamic vinegar

3/4 cup water

3/4 cup sugar

1/4 cup unsalted butter

TOPPING

2 large strawberries, hulled and sliced

2 (1/2-pint) containers blueberries

1 (1/2-pint) container raspberries

SERVES 8

*For the crust*: Combine flour, sugar, and salt in a processor; blend 5 seconds. Add butter and blend, pulsing, until coarse meal forms. Add egg yolk and cream. Pulse until moist clumps form. Gather dough into a ball. Press dough evenly into a 9-inch tart pan with a removable bottom. Pierce dough all over with a fork. Chill 1 hour.

Preheat oven to 375 degrees F. Bake crust until golden, pressing with the back of a fork if crust bubbles, about 22 minutes. Cool.

*For the filling*: Stir cream and cornstarch in a medium bowl until cornstarch dissolves. Add eggs, yolks, and vanilla; whisk to blend.

Boil vinegar in a heavy medium saucepan until reduced to 1/4 cup, about 3 minutes. Add water, sugar, and butter. Stir until butter melts; return to a boil. Gradually whisk vinegar mixture into egg mixture; return to pan. Whisk custard until it thickens and boils, about 1 minute. Strain into a bowl; cool. Spread custard in the prepared crust. Cover and chill tart at least 3 hours and up to 1 day.

*For the topping*: Mix the berries and spread over the tart when ready to serve.

# Rustic Raspberry Tart with Butter Crust

CRUST

1 cup flour

1/4 teaspoon salt

6 tablespoons cold unsalted
  butter

1 large egg, separated

3 to 5 teaspoons ice water

FILLING

2 cups raspberries

3 tablespoons sugar

2 teaspoons cornstarch

SERVES 4 TO 6

*For the crust*: Preheat oven to 425 degrees F. In a food processor, combine flour and salt. Add butter, pulsing until mixture resembles coarse meal. Slowly add egg yolk and water, 1 teaspoon at a time; process just until dough clumps together and begins to form a ball. Gather dough and place on flour-dusted plastic wrap cut into a 15-inch-long section. Flatten into a disk about 6 inches wide. Place another piece of 15-inch plastic wrap, floured-side down, on top of dough. With rolling pin, flatten into an even, 11- to 12-inch round; lift and smooth plastic wrap and continue rolling, as needed. Remove top sheet of wrap and invert dough into a 15 x 2-inch baking sheet lined with cooking parchment paper. Remove remaining plastic wrap.

*For the filling:* Place the raspberries in the center of the pastry, leaving about a 2-inch border. In a small bowl, mix sugar and cornstarch. Sprinkle 3 tablespoons mixture evenly over fruit. Gently fold edges of pastry over berries, pleating edges; leave an opening 4 to 6 inches wide in the center. Brush pastry with egg white, the sprinkle with remaining sugar mixture.

Bake tart on the bottom rack of the oven until crust is golden and juices bubble, 25 to 30 minutes. Cool on the pan at least 15 minutes. While still warm, lift tart from the pan with a wide spatula and transfer to a serving platter. Serve warm or cool. Dust tart with confectioners' sugar, if desired, or serve with vanilla ice cream or topped with whipped cream.

# Chocolate-Raspberry Fudge Tart

Pastry for a 9-inch pie

1/2 cup unsalted butter

4 ounces semisweet chocolate,
  cut up

3/4 cup sugar

2 eggs

1 egg yolk

1/2 teaspoon vanilla

1/4 cup half-and-half or light
  cream

2 to 3 tablespoons raspberry jam,
  melted

Fresh raspberries, for garnish

SERVES 8

Preheat oven to 450 degrees F. Line a 9-inch tart pan with a removable bottom or a pie plate with the pastry. Line the pastry with heavy foil and fill with pie weights, beans, or rice. Bake for 10 minutes. Remove and cool; reduce oven temperature to 325 degrees F. When cooled, remove foil and pie weights.

In a heavy saucepan, melt butter and chocolate over low heat. Stir in sugar, eggs, yolk, and vanilla until mixture is smooth. Stir in half-and-half. Pour mixture into prepared pie shell. Bake for 25 to 30 minutes, or until the tart's center is nearly set when you shake it. Cool tart on a wire rack, then remove the rim. Brush the cooled tart with melted raspberry jam. Store the tart in the refrigerator. To serve, arrange fresh raspberries decoratively on top of the tart.

# Chocolate-Raspberry Tartlets

1-3/4 cups flour

1/4 cup unsweetened cocoa
powder

1/2 teaspoon salt

1/2 cup unsalted butter, at room
temperature

1/2 cup sugar

1 large egg

1 teaspoon vanilla

FILLING

3/4 cup sugar

2 tablespoons cornstarch

12 ounces bittersweet or semisweet chocolate, chopped

6 tablespoons unsalted butter

2 large eggs

2 large egg yolks

1 teaspoon Grand Marnier or
other orange liqueur (optional)

6 teaspoons raspberry jam

1 (6-ounce) container fresh
raspberries

Sweetened whipped cream, for
garnish

SERVES 6

*For the crust*: Preheat oven to 375 degrees F. Butter bottoms and sides of six (4-1/2-inch) tartlet pans with removable bottoms. Sift flour, cocoa, and salt into a medium bowl; set aside. Using an electric mixer, beat butter and sugar in a large bowl until light and creamy. Add egg and vanilla; beat until smooth. Add flour mixture and beat at low speed just until dough forms. Shape dough into a 6-inch-long log, then cut log crosswise into 6 equal rounds. Chill for an hour. Roll out each dough round on a lightly floured surface to a 6-inch round. Press 1 round over the bottom and up the sides of each prepared pan, folding edges to form double-thick sides. Pierce crusts with a fork. Refrigerate until cold, about 30 minutes. Bake crusts until set around the edges, about 8 minutes. Cool in pans on a rack. Crusts can be made 1 day ahead. Cover and store at room temperature.

*For the filling*: Preheat oven to 350 degrees F. Sift sugar and cornstarch into a small bowl. Stir chocolate and butter in the top of a double boiler over simmering water until melted and smooth. Remove from over water. Stir in cornstarch mixture. Whisk eggs and egg yolks to blend in a medium bowl; stir into chocolate mixture. Mix in liqueur.

Spoon 1 teaspoon jam into the center of each prepared crust. Arrange raspberries in crusts, dividing equally and spacing evenly. Spoon chocolate mixture over berries. Bake until filling puffs around edges, about 28 minutes. Cool 10 minutes. Remove the sides from the tartlets pans and place on dessert plates. Garnish with whipped cream.

Jozef G. Bakos (1891–1977), *The Springtime Rainbow*, 1923. Oil on canvas, 29-1/2 x 35-1/2 in. Collection of New Mexico Museum of Art. Gift of the artist in honor of Teresa Bakos, 1974. Photograph by Blair Clark.

# Toasted Coconut Cream Pie

4 eggs, separated

5 tablespoons sugar

1/3 cup milk

1 envelope unflavored gelatin

2 teaspoons vanilla

1/8 teaspoon salt

1/8 teaspoon cream of tartar

3 tablespoons sugar

2 cups whipping cream

4 tablespoons cognac

3/4 cup apricot preserves

2 tablespoons orange liqueur

1 prebaked 10-inch pie crust

1 3/4 cups finely shredded fresh coconut

SERVES 8

Place egg yolks and sugar in the top of a double boiler; beat with a whisk until lemon colored. Set top of double boiler just over simmering water, but not touching water. Cook 5 minutes, stirring constantly. Stir in milk and gelatin until gelatin is completely dissolved. Remove from heat and transfer to a large bowl. Mix in vanilla. Allow to cool.

Beat egg whites with an electric mixer until foamy. Add salt and cream of tartar. Continue beating until soft peaks form. Add sugar, 1 tablespoon at a time, and continue beating until peaks are stiff and shiny but not dry. Fold into cooled egg yolk mixture.

Whip cream until soft peaks form; add cognac and beat until stiff. Fold into egg mixture.

Whirl apricot preserves and orange liqueur in a blender to make a glaze. Coat the baked shell with apricot glaze using a pastry brush. Spoon the filling into the crust and refrigerate pie until firm.

To serve, preheat oven to 350 degrees F. Spread coconut on a baking sheet. Bake 5 to 6 minutes, until lightly browned, stirring often to prevent uneven browning. Sprinkle pie with toasted coconut.

# Pineapple Tart

3 (2-1/2-inch-square) graham
  crackers

1-1/2 tablespoons sugar

4 (17 x 12-inch) phyllo dough
  sheets, thawed, stacked between
  wax paper and covered with a
  kitchen towel

2 tablespoons unsalted butter,
  melted

FILLING

1 large ripe pineapple, peeled,
  halved lengthwise, cored, and
  cut crosswise into 1/4-inch-
  thick slices

1/4 cup firmly packed light brown
  sugar

1/4 cup sugar

1/2 vanilla bean, seeds scraped,
  pod reserved

SERVES 8

*For the tart shell*: Preheat oven to 375 degrees F. Coat an 11-inch tart pan with a removable bottom with cooking spray. In a food processor, process graham crackers with sugar to fine crumbs. Working quickly, line a tart pan with 1 phyllo sheet, allowing edges to overhang evenly; dab butter with a pastry brush over phyllo in several places. Sprinkle with a third of the crumb mixture. Top with another phyllo sheet, placing it over the first sheet at right angles so that the overhang is even. Dab phyllo sheet again with butter and sprinkle with a third of the crumb mixture. Repeat layering with the remaining 2 phyllo sheets in the same manner; dab with butter and sprinkle with the remaining crumb mixture, ending with a phyllo sheet on top. Trim dough overhang 1-inch and turn excess inward to form a slight edge inside the tart pan. Brush shell with the remaining butter. Bake in the oven for 12 minutes, or until golden. Cool shell in tart pan on a wire rack. Shell may be made 1 day ahead up to this point, and stored, covered loosely, in a cool dry place.

*For the filling*: In a heavy 12-inch skillet, simmer pineapple slices, sugars, vanilla seeds, and vanilla pod over moderate heat. Turn pineapple slices in the skillet without breaking and lower the heat as the liquid evaporates. Continue until most of the liquid is gone and pineapple is translucent. Cool filling a bit and remove vanilla pod.

Arrange pineapple in overlapping concentric circles in pastry shell and top with any remaining syrup in skillet. Tart may be made 1 day ahead and kept, covered loosely, at room temperature.

The Aguilar Family, *Baptismal Scene*, c. 1960. Ocotlán de Morelos, Oaxaca, Mexico. Painted earthenware. Girard Foundation Collection. Museum of International Folk Art. Photograph by Michael Monteaux. A.1979.53.137.

# Pecan and Piñon Pie

## CRUST

1-1/3 cups flour

1 tablespoon sugar

1/2 teaspoon salt

6 tablespoons chilled unsalted butter, cut into 1/2-inch cubes

2 tablespoons solid vegetable shortening, frozen, cut into small pieces

3 tablespoons ice water, as needed

## FILLING

1 cup sugar

4 large eggs

2/3 cup light corn syrup

1/2 cup dark corn syrup

1-1/2 tablespoons flour

1/8 teaspoon salt

1/4 cup unsalted butter, melted and cooled

1 cup pecan halves

2/3 cup piñons

1 large egg white, beaten to blend

Sweetened whipped cream for garnish

*For the crust*: Blend flour, sugar, and salt in a food processor for a few seconds. Cut in butter and shortening using on/off turns, or pulses, until mixture forms pea-size pieces. Add 2-1/2 tablespoons ice water. Blend until moist clumps form, adding more water if dough is dry. Form dough into a ball; flatten into disk shape. Wrap in plastic wrap and store in the refrigerator at least 1 hour or overnight.

*For the filling*: Whisk first 6 ingredients in a medium bowl until smooth. Add butter and continue whisking until blended. Stir in nuts.

Preheat oven to 350 degrees F with the rack positioned in the lower third of the oven. Roll out dough to a 13-inch circle on a lightly floured work surface. Transfer to a 9-inch glass pie pan. Fold overhang under and crimp edges. Brush egg white on the bottom and sides of the crust (not edges). Pour in filling. Bake pie until filling is set and crust is golden, about 1 hour. Cool on a rack. Serve with whipped cream.

Pie can be made 8 hours ahead and kept at room temperature.

# Sweet Potato Tart

## CRUST

1-1/2 cups flour

3/4 cups whole almonds, lightly toasted

1/2 teaspoon salt

1/2 cup unsalted butter, at room temperature

1/3 cup confectioners' sugar

1 large egg

## FILLING

1 (1-pound) sweet potato (red-skinned)

3/4 cup sugar

1/2 cup whipping cream

2 large eggs

1 teaspoon vanilla

1/2 teaspoon ground cinnamon

1/4 teaspoon ground ginger

1/4 teaspoon ground nutmeg

1/8 teaspoon salt

1 cup mini marshmallows

1/2 cup chopped pecans, toasted

Sweetened whipped cream for garnish

SERVES 8 TO 10

*For the crust*: Process flour, almonds, and salt in a processor until almonds are finely ground; set aside. Beat butter and confectioners' sugar in a large bowl with an electric mixer until light and fluffy. Add egg and beat until just blended. Gradually add flour mixture, beating until moist clumps form. Form dough into a ball; then flatten to a disk. Chill dough at least 1 hour or overnight.

Roll out slightly softened dough on a lightly floured work surface to a 14-inch circle. Transfer to a 10-inch tart pan with a removable bottom. Pierce bottom of tart shell with a fork. Return to refrigerator to chill for 1 hour.

Preheat oven to 325 degrees F. Bake tart shell about 25 minutes, until lightly golden. Place on a wire rack to cool completely.

*For the filling*: Preheat oven to 375 degrees F. Roast sweet potato on a foil-lined baking sheet until very tender, about 45 minutes. Halve sweet potato lengthwise; when cool enough to handle, scoop out pulp. Place 1 cup sweet potato pulp into a blender (remaining pulp can be saved for another use). Add sugar, cream, eggs, vanilla, spices, and salt and blend until smooth. Sprinkle mini marshmallows and pecans over baked tart crust. Pour filling into crust. Bake tart until filling is set, about 35 minutes. Transfer to a wire rack to cool. To serve, cold or at room temperature, top with sweetened whipped cream.

Tart can be made 1 day ahead, covered and refrigerated.

# Creamy Dessert Finales

## Apricot Bread Pudding with Caramel Sauce

### BREAD PUDDING

1 cup Grand Marnier or other orange liqueur

1/4 cup water

5 cups whipping cream

6 large eggs

1 cup sugar

1 tablespoon vanilla extract

1/2 teaspoon grated nutmeg

8 croissants, cubed (about 1 pound)

1 cup diced dried apricots

### SAUCE

1 cup sugar

2 tablespoons water

2 tablespoons light corn syrup

1/2 cup whipping cream

1/4 cup unsalted butter

1/2 teaspoon vanilla extract

**SERVES 12**

*For the bread pudding*: Preheat oven to 350 degrees F. Simmer liqueur and water in a heavy medium saucepan for 5 minutes; cool completely. Whisk liqueur, cream, eggs, sugar, vanilla, and nutmeg in a large bowl to blend. Place croissant pieces in 9 x 13-inch glass baking dish. Add apricots and toss to combine. Pour custard over croissant-apricot mixture, pressing down gently with a rubber spatula so that all ingredients are covered evenly. Let stand 20 minutes.

Cover baking dish with aluminum foil. Place dish in a larger roasting pan; add enough hot water to the roasting pan to come 1 inch up the sides of baking dish. Bake 1 hour. Remove aluminum foil and continue baking until bread pudding is golden brown on top and firm to the touch, about 30 minutes longer. Remove from oven and cool slightly.

*For the sauce*: Stir sugar, water, and corn syrup in a heavy medium saucepan over medium to low heat until sugar dissolves. Increase heat; boil without stirring until syrup turns deep amber, brushing down the sides of the pan with a wet pastry brush and swirling the pan occasionally, about 8 minutes. Remove from heat. Whisk in cream, butter, and vanilla (the mixture will bubble vigorously). Place pan over low heat and stir until sauce thickens slightly, about 2 minutes. Cover and chill. Makes about 1-1/2 cups. Can be prepared 1 day ahead. Rewarm over medium-low heat before serving.

Drizzle bread pudding with caramel sauce if desired and serve warm.

*Croissants and Grand Marnier custard make this bread pudding super decadent. It's great with, or without, the caramel sauce. If you are short on time, substitute a purchased sauce.*

Edward Kemp, *Flower Garden at San Gabriel Ranch, Alcalde, NM*, c. 1910–1920. Collection of the Palace of the Governors Photo Archives.

# Baked Apple Custard
## with Caramel Pepper Sauce

**CUSTARD**

4 large Golden Delicious apples

3 eggs

1 cup milk

1/2 cup whipping cream

1 teaspoon vanilla extract

2 tablespoons plus 2 teaspoons
    sugar, divided

1/2 teaspoon ground cinnamon

**SAUCE**

7 tablespoons sugar

6 tablespoons hot water, divided

1/2 cup whipping cream

1 teaspoon freshly ground black
    pepper

2 tablespoons Calvados, or other
    apple brandy

*For the custard*: Preheat oven to 300 degrees F. Remove the core and seeds from the apples; peel and halve them lengthwise. Cut crosswise into thin slices. Arrange 1 apple in an overlapping flower pattern in a 6-inch shallow gratin or baking dish. Repeat to fill 3 more dishes. Blend together the eggs, milk, cream, vanilla, and 2 tablespoons sugar. Spoon gently over the apples, distributing evenly among the four dishes. Mix the remaining sugar with the cinnamon. Sprinkle evenly over the apples, coating lightly. Arrange dishes in a roasting pan. Set in the center of the oven and pour in boiling water to reach halfway up the sides of the baking dishes. Bake until the custard has just set in the center, 30 to 35 minutes.

*For the sauce*: Combine sugar and 3 tablespoons hot water in a small heavy-bottomed pan; let stand a few minutes to moisten evenly. Cook over low heat until the sugar dissolves completely. Cover and continue to cook for an additional minute to be sure all crystals have washed down the sides. Raise the heat and swirl the pan until the syrup turns medium amber. Remove from heat and drizzle in remaining hot water, keeping clear of considerable splatters. Return to heat and stir a moment until the caramel has completely dissolved. Add the cream and pepper and simmer for 2 minutes. Cool to lukewarm. Strain through a sieve; add the brandy. Chill.

Serve warm apple custard with the caramel pepper sauce alongside.

*If the sauce is chilled, the pepper flavor becomes pleasantly pronounced; however, if served at room temperature, it helps retain the appealing warmth of the custard.*

# Bananas Foster Bread Pudding
## with Vanilla Ice Cream and Caramel Sauce

SERVES 10 TO 12

### PUDDING

9 tablespoons unsalted butter, divided

1-1/2 cups firmly packed light brown sugar, divided

3/4 teaspoon ground cinnamon

6 firm, ripe bananas, peeled and sliced

1/4 cup banana liqueur

1/2 cup dark rum

4 large eggs, lightly beaten

3 cups heavy cream

1 cup milk

1 teaspoon vanilla

Pinch of salt

6 cups (1/2-inch cubes) day-old French bread

Vanilla ice cream

### SAUCE

3/4 cup sugar

2 tablespoons water

1/2 teaspoon fresh lemon juice

1/2 cup heavy cream

2 tablespoons to 1/4 cup whole milk

*For the bread pudding*: Preheat oven to 350 degrees F. Butter a 10 x 14-inch baking dish with 1 tablespoon of the butter and set aside. Melt the remaining butter in a large skillet over medium heat. Add 1 cup brown sugar and the cinnamon and cook, stirring, until the sugar dissolves, about 2 minutes. Add the bananas and cook on both sides, turning, until the bananas start to soften and brown, about 3 minutes. Add the banana liqueur and stir to blend. Carefully add the rum and shake the pan back and forth to warm the rum and flame the pan. (Or, off the heat, carefully ignite the rum with a match and return to the heat.) Shake the pan back and forth, basting the bananas, until the flame dies. Remove from heat and let cool.

Whisk together eggs, remaining brown sugar, cream, milk, vanilla, and salt in a large bowl. Add the cooled banana mixture and bread and stir to blend thoroughly. Pour into the prepared baking dish and bake until firm, 50 minutes to 1 hour. Cool on a wire rack for 20 minutes.

*For the sauce*: Combine the sugar, water, and lemon juice in a medium heavy saucepan and cook, stirring, over medium-high heat until the sugar dissolves. Let boil without stirring until the mixture becomes a deep amber color, 2 to 3 minutes, watching closely so it doesn't burn. Carefully add the cream (it may splatter), whisk to combine, and remove from heat. Add the milk, 2 tablespoons at a time, until the desired consistency is reached. Remove from the heat and let cool to room temperature before serving.

The sauce will thicken as it cools. Yields a generous 3/4 cup caramel sauce.

To serve, place a scoop of the warm pudding onto dessert plates. Top each serving with a small dollop of vanilla ice cream, drizzle with caramel sauce, and serve immediately.

# Chilled Mocha Soufflé

2 ounces semisweet chocolate

4 teaspoons instant espresso
coffee crystals

3 large eggs

6 egg yolks

1 cup sugar

1 tablespoon unflavored gelatin

2 tablespoons brewed coffee, at
room temperature

2 cups whipping cream

Coffee-flavored liqueur

SERVES 8

Melt chocolate. Stir in coffee crystals and set aside. In the top of a double boiler, combine and heat eggs, yolks, and sugar. Transfer to a bowl and beat with an electric mixer until a light color. Stir in chocolate mixture. Dissolve gelatin in room temperature coffee. Add to chocolate mixture. Beat 3 minutes with an electric mixer. Cool.

Whip cream and fold into the mixture. Pour into a 1-quart soufflé dish. Refrigerate. Serve with coffee-flavored liqueur.

# Chocolate Bread Pudding with
# Sun-Dried Cherries and Crème Fraîche

1/2 cup sun-dried cherries

1/3 cup cognac

1/2 loaf French baguette

8 ounces bittersweet chocolate

3 eggs

1 cup cream

1/2 cup sour cream

1/2 cup sugar

1/4 teaspoon ground cinnamon

1 teaspoon vanilla

1 cup crème fraîche

1 tablespoon confectioners' sugar

SERVES 6

Preheat oven to 350 degrees F. Soak the cherries in cognac for 1 hour.

Remove the crust from the baguette and cut the center of the bread into small cubes. Place the cubed bread on a baking sheet and toast lightly in the oven.

In a medium-size mixing bowl, melt the chocolate in a double boiler. In another mixing bowl, mix the eggs, cream, sour cream, sugar, cinnamon, and vanilla. Pour this mixture into the melted chocolate and mix well to incorporate thoroughly. Add the soaked cherries and cognac, and the toasted cubed bread. Set the bowl aside for about 2 hours in order to let the bread absorb the mixture well.

Pour the mixture into six 8- to 10-ounce ramekins. Place the ramekins in a baking pan and add enough hot water to come halfway up the sides. Cover the pan loosely with foil and bake until the pudding is just set, about 35 minutes. The pudding should be soft in the center when lightly shaken. Remove from the oven. In a small bowl, whip the crème fraîche with the confectioners' sugar. Serve pudding hot with a dollop of the crème fraîche.

# Chocolate Raisin Bread Pudding

1 (1-pound) loaf unsliced white sandwich bread

4 large eggs

1 cup whole milk

1 cup heavy cream

1 cup half-and-half

1 cup sugar

1/4 cup unsweetened cocoa powder, sifted

1/2 teaspoon vanilla

1/2 teaspoon salt

1/2 cup semisweet chocolate chips

1/2 cup golden raisins

Purchased chocolate sauce and whipped cream topping for garnish

SERVES 8

Preheat oven to 350 degrees F. Cut bread into 1-inch cubes making 8 cups of cubes. Whisk together eggs, milk, cream, half-and-half, sugar, cocoa, vanilla, and salt in a large bowl. Stir in bread until coated and let stand 5 minutes. Stir in chocolate chips and raisins, and transfer pudding to a buttered 9 x 13-inch baking pan. Bake pudding in a water bath in the middle of the oven until custard is just set, about 40 minutes. Serve warm.

Garnish with a purchased chocolate sauce and whipped cream.

*Any unsweetened cocoa powder will work well, but for the richest, darkest pudding, use Valrhona.*

# Panna Cottas with Raspberry Sauce

PANNA COTTAS

1-1/2 teaspoons unflavored gelatin

6 tablespoons milk

1-2/3 cups heavy cream

1/4 cup sugar

3/4 teaspoon vanilla

Pinch of salt

RASPBERRY SAUCE

1/3 cup sugar

2 tablespoons fresh lemon juice

1/3 cup plus 2 tablespoons water, divided

6 ounces frozen raspberries or 1-1/4 cups thawed (not in syrup)

1 teaspoon cornstarch

SERVES 6

*For the panna cottas:* Sprinkle gelatin over milk in a bowl and let stand until softened, about 2 minutes. Heat cream and sugar in a heavy saucepan over moderate heat, stirring constantly, until sugar is dissolved and mixture registers 160 degrees F on an instant-read thermometer. Stir cream into milk mixture until gelatin is dissolved, then stir in vanilla and salt. Pour into six (4- to 5-ounce) oiled ramekins and chill, covered, at least 8 hours.

*For the raspberry sauce:* Bring sugar, lemon juice, and 1/3 cup water to a boil in a small saucepan. Simmer for 2 minutes while stirring. Add raspberries and return to a boil. Remove from the heat and cool, covered, for 10 minutes. Force raspberry mixture through a fine sieve into another saucepan. Stir together cornstarch and the remaining water, then stir into the raspberry sauce. Bring to a boil over moderate heat; boil for 2 minutes, stirring constantly. Transfer to a bowl and chill, covered, until cold, about 4 hours.

To serve, run a sharp knife around the edge of the ramekins, then briefly dip ramekins in warm water, about 30 seconds. Invert onto plates and serve with raspberry sauce. Panna cottas can chill up to 3 days.

# Vanilla Flan

3/4 cup sugar

1 (14-ounce) can sweetened condensed milk

1 cup whipping cream

1/2 cup milk

4 eggs

1 cinnamon stick

SERVES 8

Preheat oven to 325 degrees F. Heat sugar in a small heavy skillet over medium-high heat. When the sugar begins to melt, reduce heat to medium or medium-low. Stir until sugar is melted and caramel colored, then quickly pour into a shallow 1-1/2-quart baking dish.

Combine condensed milk, cream, milk, and eggs in a blender and process until thoroughly mixed. Pour over caramelized sugar in baking dish. Insert cinnamon stick into the middle of the flan mixture. Place the baking dish in a large baking pan and fill the pan with hot water halfway up the sides. Bake 1 hour and 50 minutes, or until a knife inserted in the center comes out clean. If the flan gets too brown on top while cooking, cover it loosely with aluminum foil. When done, remove the baking dish from the pan of hot water. Cool, then refrigerate for 3 to 4 hours.

To serve, run a knife around the edge of the flan and invert the dish onto a serving plate.

# Warm Chocolate Risotto

1 cup Arborio rice

2 cups water

4 cups half-and-half, heated

6 ounces bittersweet chocolate, chopped

1 tablespoon vanilla extract

2 tablespoons sugar

SERVES 4 TO 6

Combine rice and water in a large saucepan and bring to a boil. Reduce heat and stir frequently until almost all the liquid has been absorbed. Gradually add 1/2 cup half-and-half and stir frequently until it is almost absorbed. Repeat with the remaining half-and-half, adding 1/2 cup at a time. At the last addition of half-and-half, add the chocolate, vanilla, and sugar, stirring constantly, until most of the half-and-half has been absorbed and the rice is tender.

Felipa Trujillo, *Cochiti Man*, c. 1960. Cochiti Pueblo, New Mexico. Slipped and painted earthenware, 10-3/4 in. high. Girard Foundation Collection. Museum of International Folk Art. Photograph by Michael Monteaux. A.1979.53.137.

# Mexican-Spiced Chocolate Bread Pudding

6 cups cubed sourdough bread, with the crusts removed

2 cups half-and-half

1 ounce Mexican chocolate, chopped

4 ounces bittersweet chocolate, coarsely chopped

1/2 cup raisins

2 large eggs

1/4 cup sugar

1/4 teaspoon ground cinnamon

Chocolate curls for garnish

SERVES 8

Cut the bread into 2-inch cubes. Spread out bread cubes and let stand until dried and firm (12 to 24 hours), or spread in a 10 x 15-inch pan and bake in a 175-degree F oven until dried and firm, about 1-1/2 hours.

Preheat oven to 350 degrees F. Place a 1- to 2-quart pan over medium-high heat; add the half-and-half, stirring often until steaming, about 5 minutes. Remove from the heat; add the Mexican chocolate, bittersweet chocolate, and raisins. Stir often until the chocolate melts.

In a bowl, beat eggs, sugar, and cinnamon to blend. Stir in milk mixture and bread. Let stand until bread is saturated 20 to 30 minutes, stirring often. Scrape mixture into a buttered shallow 2- to 2-1/2-quart casserole; cover tightly with foil.

Set casserole in a pan that is at least 2 inches deep and 2 inches wider than the casserole. Place the casserole in the center of the oven and pour 1 inch of boiling water into the pan. Bake covered for 15 minutes. Uncover the casserole and bake 15 to 20 minutes, until pudding center is set and the bread feels slightly firm when pressed. Serve hot or warm.

Garnish with chocolate curls.

*If Mexican chocolate is unavailable, mix 1 ounce chopped bittersweet chocolate with 2 tablespoons sugar and 1/4 teaspoon ground cinnamon.*

# Orange Crème Brulée

2 cups heavy cream

4 egg yolks

1/4 cup sugar

1/2 teaspoon grated orange zest

3 tablespoons orange juice

1/3 cup brown sugar, sifted

SERVES 6

Preheat oven to 325 degrees F. In a medium saucepan scald cream. Meanwhile, in a medium bowl, whisk yolks and sugar until thick and light. Slowly pour in hot cream, whisking constantly. Return mixture to the saucepan and cook over medium-low heat, stirring constantly, until mixture coats the back of a spoon, about 10 minutes. Remove from heat. Add zest and juice. Pour into 6 individual ramekins.

Place ramekins in a baking pan, fill pan with hot water halfway up the sides of the ramekins. Bake 20 minutes, or until centers are set. Cool on a wire rack. Place in the freezer for 15 minutes, or cover loosely with plastic wrap and refrigerate overnight.

To serve, preheat broiler. Sprinkle custard evenly with brown sugar. Broil until sugar is melted and a thin crust forms, about 3 minutes.

# Spanish Cream

3 cups milk

1 tablespoon gelatin

1/2 cup sugar

3 egg yolks, slightly beaten

1/4 teaspoon salt

1 teaspoon vanilla

3 egg whites, stiffly beaten

Whipped cream for topping

SERVES 6

Scald milk with gelatin; add sugar and pour slowly on egg yolks. Place mixture in a double boiler and cook, stirring constantly, until the mixture coats spoon; remove from heat.

Fold in salt, vanilla, and egg whites. Turn into 6 individual ramekins, first dipped in cold water; chill.

To serve, top with whipped cream.

# Crêpes de Cajeta con Nuez

## CRÊPES

2-1/2 cups milk

5 large eggs

1 cup flour

6 tablespoons unsalted butter, melted and cooled

2 tablespoons sugar

3/4 teaspoon salt

## SAUCE

3 cups cajeta (Mexican caramelized goat or cow milk)

3/4 cup milk

3 tablespoons unsalted butter

3 tablespoons cognac or brandy

2 cups pecans, toasted and chopped

SERVES 12

*For the crêpes:* Combine ingredients in a blender and blend until smooth. Let stand 1 hour at room temperature.

Heat a buttered 8- to 9-inch-diameter nonstick skillet over medium-high heat. Pour a scant 1/4 cup batter into skillet, tilting to allow batter to coat the bottom of the skillet. Cook until crêpe is golden on bottom, about 1 minute. Turn crêpe over and cook until brown on the bottom, about 45 seconds. Transfer to a paper towel. Repeat with remaining batter, making 24 crêpes, stacking them between paper towels. Cool.

*For the sauce:* Combine cajeta, milk, and butter in a heavy medium saucepan. Bring to a boil. Reduce heat to medium and simmer until sauce is reduced to 2-3/4 cups, about 5 minutes. Remove from heat. Stir in cognac.

Place 1 crêpe on work surface; spread with 1 tablespoon sauce. Sprinkle with 1 tablespoon of chopped pecans. Fold crêpe in half over filling and then in half again, forming a triangle. Repeat with remaining crêpes, sauce, and pecans. Arrange crêpes in two 9 x 13-inch glass baking dishes. Can be prepared 1 day ahead. Cover and chill crêpes and remaining sauce separately. Rewarm sauce just until pourable.

Preheat oven to 350 degrees F. Pour warm sauce over crêpes. Bake until heated through, about 15 minutes. Divide and serve on individual warm dessert plates. Sprinkle with any remaining pecans.

# Postre para los Angeles

2 large eggs

1 cup sugar

1/2 cup fine breadcrumbs

1 cup chopped dates

1 cup chopped almonds or pecans

2 teaspoons vanilla, divided

1 teaspoon baking powder

2 cups whipping cream

1/2 cup confectioners' sugar

SERVES 6 TO 8

Prepare 5 to 7 days ahead. Beat eggs until fluffy. Add sugar and beat until very light and fluffy. Add breadcrumbs, dates, nuts, 1 teaspoon vanilla, and baking powder and mix well. Pour into an 8 x 8-inch square greased and floured pan. Bake for 20 minutes, or until a tester inserted comes out clean. Let stand uncovered for 5 to 7 days to completely dry out, then crumble into small chunks.

To serve, beat whipping cream with confectioners' sugar and the remaining vanilla until soft, firm peaks are formed. Fold in small chunks of the dried bread and serve in dessert dishes.

*The recipe for this 170-year-old traditional New Mexican Christmas dessert came from Bernadette Pesenti-Valdes' great-grandmother.*

# Andiamo's Panna Cotta

1-3/4 cups sugar

Juice of 1/2 lemon

5 cups heavy cream

1/2 cup sugar

1 tablespoon vanilla

1/4 teaspoon almond extract

1-1/2 teaspoons gelatin

1/4 cup water

2 cups shredded unsweetened coconut, lightly toasted

SERVES 8 TO 10

Place sugar in a small pan with just enough water to cover. Carmelize sugar until dark but not burnt. Pour enough into ramekins to coat the bottom of 8 to 10 ramekins.

Heat lemon juice, cream, sugar, vanilla, and almond extract just enough to melt the sugar. In a separate pan add gelatin to the water. Let it expand.

Heat gelatin just until it turns to liquid. (Do not let gelatin boil!) Mix gelatin and coconut with cream mixture. Pour mixture into individual ramekins and let set 4 to 6 hours before serving.

—*Joan Gillcrist, Owner, Andiamo Restaurant*

Campbell Hotel Chicago Slide Co., *Indian Country*, c. 1910–1920, Collection of the Palace of the Governors Photo Archives.

# Lemon-Buttermilk Panna Cotta with Blueberry Sauce

PANNA COTTA

1-1/2 tablespoons unflavored gelatin

1 cup whole milk

1/2 cup plus 2 tablespoons sugar

3 cups low-fat buttermilk

1 teaspoon grated lemon zest

BLUEBERRY SAUCE

1/2 cup apple juice

1/4 cup sugar

1 tablespoon fresh lemon juice

2 cups blueberries

Mint sprigs, optional

SERVES 8

*For the panna cotta:* Coat eight (6-ounce) custard cups with cooking spray. Sprinkle gelatin over whole milk in a small saucepan; let stand 10 minutes. Cook milk mixture over medium-low heat 10 minutes, or until gelatin dissolves, stirring constantly with a whisk. Increase heat to medium, add sugar, stirring with a whisk until sugar dissolves. Remove from heat. Add buttermilk and zest, stirring well. Divide mixture evenly among prepared custard cups. Cover and chill at least 5 hours, or up to overnight.

*For the blueberry sauce:* Combine the apple juice, sugar, and lemon juice in a small saucepan. Bring to a boil over medium-high heat; stir until sugar dissolves. Reduce heat to medium; stir in blueberries. Cook 8 minutes, or until blueberries are warm and begin to pop. Cool sauce to room temperature.

Place a dessert plate, upside down, on top of each custard cup, then invert panna cotta onto plates. Serve with blueberry sauce.

Garnish with mint sprigs, if desired.

# Cheesecakes Deliciosos

## Strawberries and Cream Cheesecake

### STRAWBERRIES
1-1/2 pounds strawberries, hulled

3 tablespoons light corn syrup

### CRUST
1-1/2 cups finely ground graham crackers (about 4 sheets)

3 tablespoons sugar

3 tablespoons unsalted butter, melted

### FILLING
1 pound plus 13 ounces cream cheese, softened

1 cup sugar

1/4 teaspoon salt

2 large eggs, at room temperature

1 vanilla bean, seeds scraped and reserved

8-3/4 ounces mascarpone cheese, at room temperature

SERVES 8 TO 10

*For the strawberries*: Preheat oven to 300 degrees F. Place strawberries in a single layer on a rimmed baking sheet. Drizzle with corn syrup and toss gently to coat. Bake until syrup thickens and strawberries turn deep red and shrink slightly, about 1-1/2 hours. Transfer strawberries and syrup to a medium bowl and mash with a potato masher; let cool completely.

*For the crust*: Increase oven temperature to 350 degrees F. Stir together graham cracker crumbs, sugar, and butter in a small bowl. Press mixture into the bottom of a 9-inch springform pan to make an even layer. Bake until the crust is firm to the touch and has just darkened, about 10 minutes. Transfer pan to a wire rack and let crust cool completely.

*For the filling*: Reduce oven temperature to 325 degrees F. Place cream cheese into the bowl of an electric mixer fitted with the paddle attachment and mix on medium-low speed until creamy, about 2 minutes. Scrape down sides of bowl, then gradually add sugar and salt. Scrape down sides of the bowl; add eggs, 1 at a time, mixing well after each addition. Scrape down sides of the bowl and mix in vanilla bean seeds and mascarpone until very creamy and with no lumps, about 3 minutes. (Reserve vanilla bean for another use.)

Transfer 5 cups cream cheese mixture to the bowl with the mashed strawberries; stir to combine. Pour strawberry-cream cheese mixture on top of crust; smooth with an offset spatula. Carefully spoon dollops of plain cream cheese mixture on top and smooth with an offset spatula.

Wrap the exterior of the springform pan in 2 layers of foil; place in a large roasting pan. Fill roasting pan with boiling water until water reaches halfway up the sides of the springform pan. Bake cheesecake until set, about 1 hour to 1 hour 10 minutes. Remove springform pan from the water bath and transfer to a wire rack to cool. Refrigerate until cold, at least 4 hours (up to overnight). To serve, run a knife around the edges and remove springform pan.

Sheldon Parsons (1866–1943), *Clouds*, c. 1943. Oil on plywood panel, 36 x 36 in. Collection of New Mexico Museum of Art. Gift of Mrs. Sarah Parsons Mack, 1948. Photograph by Blair Clark.

# Caramel-Toffee Cheesecake

1-1/2 cups ground gingersnap
cookies

5 tablespoons unsalted butter,
melted

2 tablespoons firmly packed light
brown sugar

CHEESECAKE

4 (8-ounce) packages cream
cheese, at room temperature

1 cup firmly packed light brown
sugar

2 tablespoons butter, melted

5 extra large eggs

1 teaspoon vanilla

CARAMEL TOPPING

1-1/2 cups sugar

1/4 cup water

1/2 teaspoon fresh lemon juice

1 cup heavy whipping cream

6 ounces English toffee bits
(such as Heath or Skor)

SERVES 8 TO 10

*For the crust*: Preheat oven to 350 degrees F. Spray bottom of a 9-inch spring-form pan with nonstick spray. Combine gingersnap crust ingredients and press into bottom (only) of pan. Crisscross three sheets of heavy-duty aluminum foil. Place springform pan on the center of the aluminum foil, wrapping the outside of the pan in the foil to a level just above the rim. Bake the crust until firm and beginning to darken, no more than 14 minutes. Cool crust, leave foil intact, and maintain oven temperature.

*For the cheesecake*: Beat cream cheese and sugar in a large bowl until smooth. Beat in butter, then eggs, 1 at a time, until just blended; beat in vanilla. Pour batter into the pan. Place pan wrapped in foil into a large roasting pan or baking dish. Add enough hot water around the springform pan to come halfway up the sides of the pan. Bake the cake in the water bath uncovered for about 1 hour 10 minutes until the sides of cake are firm and cake moves only slightly in the center when gently shaken.

*For the topping*: Stir sugar, water, and lemon juice in a large saucepan over medium heat until sugar dissolves. Increase heat; boil without stirring until mixture turns deep amber but not brown, occasionally swirling pan and brushing down the sides with a wet pastry brush—about 9 minutes in all up to this point. Add the cream (mixture will bubble to the top of the pan). Reduce heat to medium-low. Simmer about 8 minutes, until reduced to 1-1/4 cups, stirring occasionally. Chill until thickened but still pourable. Spoon caramel over the top of the cheesecake (do not allow the caramel to drip down the sides). Garnish the top edges with chopped English toffee. Chill at least 2 hours and up to 6 hours.

To serve, run a knife around the pan sides to loosen cake and then release pan sides.

Unidentified photographer, *Pueblo woman baking bread in a horno*, c. 1910–1920. Collection of the Palace of the Governors Photo Archives.

# Mascarpone Cheesecake with Almond Crust

**CRUST**

1 cup slivered almonds, lightly toasted

2/3 cup graham cracker crumbs

3 tablespoons sugar

1 tablespoon unsalted butter, melted

**FILLING**

2 (8-ounce) packages cream cheese, at room temperature

2 (8-ounce) containers mascarpone cheese, at room temperature

1-1/4 cups sugar

2 teaspoons fresh lemon juice

1 teaspoon vanilla

4 large eggs, at room temperature

**TOPPING**

1/2 cup chocolate-hazelnut spread (Nutella recommended)

1/4 cup whipping cream

SERVES 12 TO 16

*For the crust*: Preheat oven to 350 degrees F. Tightly wrap the outside of a 9-inch springform pan with 3 layers of heavy-duty aluminum foil. Finely grind the almonds, cracker crumbs, and sugar in a food processor. Add the butter and process until moist crumbs form. Press the almond mixture onto the bottom of the prepared pan (not on the sides of the pan). Bake the crust until it is set and beginning to brown, about 12 minutes; cool. Decrease the oven temperature to 325 degrees F.

*For the filling*: Using an electric mixer, beat the cream cheese, mascarpone, and sugar in a large bowl until smooth, occasionally scraping down the sides of the bowl with a rubber spatula. Beat in the lemon juice and vanilla. Add the eggs, 1 at a time, beating just until blended after each addition.

Pour the cheese mixture over the crust in the pan. Place the foil-wrapped springform pan in a large roasting pan. Pour enough hot water into the roasting pan to come halfway up the sides of the springform pan. Bake until the center of the cheesecake moves slightly when the pan is gently shaken, about 1 hour 5 minutes (the cake will become firm when it is cold). Transfer the cake to a rack; cool for 1 hour. Refrigerate until the cheesecake is cold, at least 8 hours and up to 2 days.

*For the topping*: Combine the chocolate-hazelnut spread and cream in a small bowl. Heat in the microwave until warm, stirring every 20 seconds to blend (about 1 minute). Cut cake into wedges and drizzle with the sauce.

# Santacafé White Chocolate Raspberry Cheesecake

## CRUST

2 cups graham cracker crumbs

1 cup slivered blanched almonds

1/4 cup clarified butter in its liquid (unchilled) form

## FILLING

8 ounces fine-quality white chocolate

4 (8-ounce) packages cream cheese, softened

1/2 cup plus 2 tablespoons sugar

4 large eggs

2 large egg yolks

2 tablespoons flour

1 teaspoon vanilla

2 pints raspberries

SERVES 8 TO 10

*For the crust*: In a food processor, blend together the graham cracker crumbs and the almonds until the almonds are ground fine; add butter and combine the mixture well. Press the mixture onto the bottom and two-thirds up the side of a 10-inch springform pan.

*For the filling*: In a metal bowl set over a pan of barely simmering water, melt the chocolate, stirring until smooth, and remove the bowl from heat. In a large bowl with an electric mixer, beat the cream cheese until it's light and fluffy; add the sugar and beat in the eggs and the yolks, adding 1 at a time and beating well after each addition. Beat in the flour and the vanilla, and add the melted chocolate in a slow stream, beating until the filling is combined well.

Scatter the raspberries over the bottom of the crust, pouring the filling over them, and bake the cheesecake in the middle of a preheated 250 degree F oven for 1 hour, or until the top is firm to the touch. Let the cheesecake cool in the pan on a rack. Chill, covered loosely, overnight; remove sides of springform pan.

—*Angel Estrada, Executive Chef, Santacafé Restaurant*

# Chocolate Chip Cheesecake

## CRUST

2/3 cup (about 3 ounces) reduced-fat chocolate wafer crumbs

1-1/2 tablespoons melted butter

## FILLING

3 (8-ounce) packages nonfat cream cheese

1 cup sugar

1 (14-ounce) can nonfat sweetened condensed milk

3 large egg whites

2 teaspoons vanilla

1 cup miniature chocolate chips, divided

SERVES 8 TO 10

*For the crust*: Combine crumbs and butter. Pat mixture evenly over bottom and about 3/4 inch up the sides of an 8- to 10-inch springform pan (at least 1-3/4 inches deep).

*For the filling*: In a food processor or bowl, whirl or beat cream cheese, sugar, condensed milk, egg whites, and vanilla until very smooth. Stir in 1/2 cup chocolate chips. Scrape batter into prepared pan. Evenly sprinkle batter with remaining chocolate chips. Bake in a 350 degree F oven until cake jiggles only slightly in the center when gently shaken, about 45 minutes.

Run a thin-bladed knife between cake and pan rim. Refrigerate cake, uncovered, until cool, at least 2-1/2 hours. Serve, or if made ahead, wrap airtight when cool and chill up to 2 days. Remove pan ring and cut cake into wedges.

# Santa Fe School of Cooking Cheesecake
## with Apricot Canela Topping

CRUST

4 whole graham crackers

1/2 cup packed dried apricots, cut into quarters

2 tablespoons sliced almonds

1/2 teaspoon ground canela (Mexican cinnamon)

FILLING

2 cups reduced-fat firm silken tofu, drained

8 ounces reduced-fat cream cheese

1/4 cup reduced-fat sour cream

2/3 cup sugar

2 large eggs

1/4 cup amaretto liqueur

Pinch of salt

APRICOT CANELA TOPPING

1 (10-ounce) jar apricot preserves

1/3 cup water

2 tablespoons amaretto liqueur

1 tablespoon freshly squeezed lemon juice

1/2 teaspoon ground canela

OPTIONAL GARNISHES

Sliced fresh apricots

Fresh blackberries

Sliced fresh peaches

Toasted sliced almonds

Mint leaves

SERVES 12

*For the crust*: Preheat oven to 325 degrees F. Coat an 8-inch springform pan with nonstick spray. Wrap the outside of pan with a double thickness of aluminum foil to keep water out while cheesecake is baking in a water bath. Place graham crackers, apricots, almonds, and canela in the bowl of a food processor and process until finely ground. Pour into prepared pan and press down evenly over bottom.

*For the filling*: Wipe crumbs from food processor and blade, and place tofu, cream cheese, sour cream, sugar, eggs, amaretto, and salt in the bowl. Process until very smooth, stopping to scrape down the sides of the bowl as needed. Pour over the crust.

Place cheesecake in a large roasting pan and pour in enough hot water to come 1 inch up the outside of the springform pan. Bake about 50 minutes, or until the edges are firm but the center still jiggles when the pan is tapped. Place cheesecake on a wire rack. Run a knife around the outer edge of the cheesecake, remove foil, and let cool to room temperature before covering and refrigerating. Make the topping just before serving.

*For the topping*: Combine all the topping ingredients in a small saucepan and cook, stirring, over low heat for 3 minutes, or until heated through. Slice cheesecake and serve each piece with apricot topping. Garnish with optional fruits or nuts as desired.

*Taken from* Southwest Flavors: Santa Fe School of Cooking, *published by Gibbs Smith, 2006.*

Anonymous artist, *Parrot*, c. 1960. Knodapalli, Andhra Pradesh, India. Painted wood, 5 in. high. Girard Foundation Collection. Museum of International Folk Art. Photograph by Michael Monteaux. A.1981.22.482.

# Orange Chocolate Swirl Cheesecake

### CRUST

1-1/2 cups vanilla wafer crumbs

1/4 cup sugar

1/3 cup butter

### FILLING

5 (8-ounce) packages cream cheese, softened

1-1/2 cups sugar

8 eggs

3 tablespoons orange juice

3/4 teaspoon grated orange zest

6 squares semisweet chocolate, melted and cooled slightly

SERVES 12

*For the crust*: Preheat oven to 325 degrees F. Mix crumbs, sugar, and butter; press onto the bottom and 1 1/2 inches up the sides of a 9-inch springform pan. Bake for 10 minutes.

*For the filling*: Beat cream cheese and sugar at medium speed with a mixer until well blended. Add eggs, 1 at a time, mixing at low speed after each addition just until blended. Blend in juice and zest.

Reserve 2 cups of the batter. Pour remaining batter over crust. Blend chocolate into reserved batter. Add spoonfuls of the chocolate batter to the cream cheese batter in the crust. Cut through the batter with a knife several times for marbled effect. Bake 55 to 60 minutes, or until center is almost set. Remove from oven and cool on a wire rack. Run a knife or metal spatula around the rim of pan to loosen the cheesecake; cool before removing rim. Refrigerate 4 hours or overnight.

# White Chocolate Cheesecake with Cranberry Swirl

**CRANBERRY MIXTURE**

1-1/2 cups fresh cranberries

3/4 cup orange juice

1/4 cup sugar

3 tablespoons dried currants

2 tablespoons Grand Marnier

1 tablespoon orange zest

1/2 teaspoon ground cinnamon

**FILLING**

6 ounces white chocolate

3 (8-ounce) packages cream cheese, softened

3/4 cup sugar

4 large eggs

Dark and white chocolate curls or shavings, optional

SERVES 8

*For the cranberry mixture:* Combine first 7 ingredients in a small saucepan. Simmer over medium heat until cranberries lose their shape and mixture thickens slightly, stirring occasionally, about 8 minutes. Transfer to a food processor and blend until smooth. Can be prepared 1 to 2 days ahead. Cover and refrigerate.

*For the filling:* Preheat oven to 350 degrees F. Stir white chocolate in the top of a double boiler over barely simmering water until melted and smooth; cool slightly. Using an electric mixer, beat cream cheese in a large bowl until smooth. Mix in sugar. Beat in eggs, 1 at a time, beating well after each addition. Gradually mix in white chocolate.

Pour half of the cream cheese filling into a 9-inch springform pan. Drop half of cranberry mixture atop in 2-tablespoon drops, spacing evenly. Use a small sharp knife to swirl cranberry mixture into filling. Carefully pour in remaining cream cheese filling. Drop remaining cranberry mixture atop in 2-tablespoon drops, spacing evenly. Use small sharp knife to swirl cranberry mixture into filling. Bake cheesecake until edges are puffed and golden and center of cheesecake moves slightly when the pan is gently shaken, about 40 minutes; cool on rack. Chill overnight. Can be prepared 3 days ahead.

Run a small sharp knife around sides to loosen cheesecake. Release pan sides. Press white chocolate curls onto edges of cheesecake if desired. Top with dark and white chocolate curls.

# Piña Colada Cheesecake

**CRUST**

3 cups finely ground vanilla wafer crumbs

1 cup shredded unsweetened coconut, divided

2 cups sugar

1/2 cup unsalted butter, melted

**FILLING**

4 (8-ounce) packages cream cheese, softened

1 cup sugar

1 teaspoon vanilla

4 eggs

2/3 cup frozen Piña Colada Tropical Fruit Mixer concentrate, thawed

SERVES 12

*For the crust:* In a large bowl, toss together the cookie crumbs, 3/4 cup coconut, and sugar. Using a fork, stir in the butter. Transfer the crumb mixture to a 9-inch springform pan and press evenly over the bottom and up the sides of the pan. Refrigerate for 15 minutes. Preheat the oven to 350 degrees F. Toast remaining coconut until lightly browned; remove from oven and cool.

*For the filling:* Mix cream cheese, sugar, and vanilla at medium speed with an electric mixer until well blended. Add eggs and mix until blended. Blend in Piña Colada mixer. Pour into pan and bake for 40 minutes, or until center is almost set. Garnish with toasted coconut.

# Isaac's Table White Chocolate Ginger Cheesecake

## CRUST

13 ounces gingersnap cookies

2 tablespoons sugar

1 tablespoon ground ginger

6-1/2 tablespoons unsalted butter, melted

## FILLING

1 pound white chocolate or 1 (16-ounce) package white chocolate chips

4 (8-ounce) packages cream cheese, softened

1/4 cup sugar

4 large eggs

1 tablespoon vanilla

1 teaspoon ground ginger

2/3 cup minced crystallized ginger

2 tablespoons cornstarch

Chocolate curls, for garnish

SERVES 12

*For the crust*: Preheat oven to 300 degrees F. Butter a 9-inch springform pan. Wrap the outside of the pan with two layers of heavy-duty aluminum foil. Finely grind cookies, sugar, and ginger in a food processor; add butter and blend until moist clumps form. Press into the bottom and up the sides of the pan. Chill 20 minutes.

*For the filling*: Melt white chocolate in a double boiler, stirring until just melted. Set aside. Using an electric mixer with a paddle (not a wire whip), beat cream cheese and sugar until fluffy, about 3 minutes. Add eggs, 1 at a time, and beat well after each addition. Add vanilla and ground ginger. Gradually add melted white chocolate. Dust minced crystallized ginger with cornstarch and add to chocolate-cream cheese mixture. Pour into chilled crust. Place wrapped springform pan in a large roasting pan filled with enough hot water to come halfway up the sides. Bake until it puffs and the edges crack slightly, about 40 minutes. After baking, leave in oven for 20 to 30 minutes, with heat turned off. Run a knife around the sides before chilling; cool completely. Chill at least 4 hours or overnight before serving. Garnish with chocolate curls if desired. Can be made up to 3 days ahead.

—*Virginia G. (Jinny) Vigil, Executive Chef, Isaac's Table, Ellis Country Store Inn*

# Amaretto Cheesecake

## CRUST

- 3/4 cup very finely crushed amaretti biscuits (18 to 20 biscuits)
- 1 tablespoon unsalted butter, melted

## FILLING

- 3 (8-ounce) packages cream cheese, at room temperature
- 3/4 cup sugar
- 4 eggs, at room temperature
- 3 tablespoons amaretto liqueur
- 1/2 teaspoon vanilla

## TOPPING

- 1 1/4 cups sour cream, at room temperature
- 2 tablespoons sugar

*For the crust*: Combine amaretti crumbs and butter in a small bowl, mixing with fingers until well blended. Reserve 1 tablespoon of mixture for later use. Press remaining crumb mixture in a very thin layer to cover the bottom and about 1/2 inch up the sides of a 10-inch springform pan. Refrigerate until cool.

*For the filling*: Beat cream cheese in a large bowl until light and fluffy, interrupting beating 2 to 3 times to scrape down the sides and beaters. Beat in 3/4 cup sugar, 2 tablespoons at a time, beating thoroughly after each addition. Beat in eggs, 1 at a time, just enough to blend thoroughly after each addition. Beat in amaretto and vanilla. Scrape mixture into prepared pan. Bake at 350 degrees F until cake begins to pull away from the sides of the pan and the center of the cake is not quite set, about 25 minutes. Remove to a wire rack and cool for 20 minutes. Maintain oven at 350 degrees F.

*For the topping*: While the cheesecake cools, combine sour cream and 2 tablespoons sugar in a small bowl. Let stand until sugar dissolves completely; stir to blend. Very carefully spread sour cream mixture in a thin smooth layer over top of cake up to, but not touching, the sides of the pan. Return cake to the oven and bake 10 minutes longer. Cool cake in the pan on a wire rack to room temperature. Sprinkle reserved 1 tablespoon amaretti crumbs in a 1/2-inch border around the edge of the cake. Refrigerate cake, lightly covered with plastic wrap, until thoroughly chilled and set—at least 2 hours. Let cake stand at room temperature for about 10 minutes before serving. This can be made way ahead as it keeps nicely in the refrigerator and is quite light.

# Heath Bar Crunch Toffee Cheesecake

MAKES 2 CAKES WITH 10 SERVINGS EACH

## CRUST

3 cups graham cracker crumbs

3/4 cup unsalted butter, melted

1/4 cup firmly packed golden brown sugar

1 teaspoon vanilla

## FILLING

2-1/2 cups coarsely crushed chocolate-covered English toffee (such as Heath or Skor, about 14 ounces)

6 (8-ounce) packages cream cheese, at room temperature

2 cups sugar

4 tablespoons vanilla

2 cups sour cream

8 large eggs

## TOPPING

3 cups sour cream

1/2 cup sugar

4 teaspoons vanilla

Chocolate-covered English toffee, coarsely chopped

Begin preparing this a day before serving. The recipe can be halved easily to make one cake.

*For the crust*: Preheat oven to 350 degrees F. Butter two 9-inch diameter springform pans with 2-3/4-inch-high sides. Blend all crust ingredients in a processor until moist. Divide mixture between prepared pans. Press onto the bottom and 2 inches up the sides of the pans.

*For the filling*: Sprinkle toffee over the bottom of each crust. Beat cream cheese, sugar, and vanilla in a large bowl until well blended. Beat in sour cream and then eggs, 1 at a time. Divide filling between prepared crusts. Bake cakes until golden on top, cracked around the edges and just set in the center, about 65 minutes. Transfer cakes to racks; let cool 10 minutes (centers will fall). Maintain oven temperature.

*For the topping*: Whisk the first 3 ingredients in a medium bowl to blend; spoon over cakes. Bake until topping just sets, about 5 minutes. Refrigerate immediately. Chill uncovered overnight. Cut around pan sides to loosen cakes. Release sides. Top with chopped toffee.

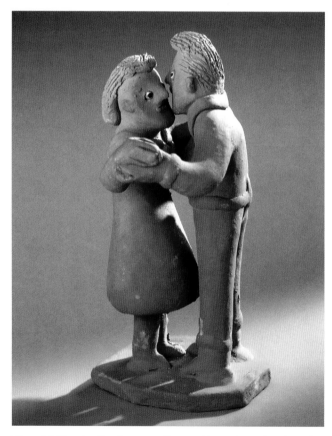

Laurel Ezequiel. *Dancing Couple*, c. 1959. Caruaru, Pernambuco, Brazil. Earthenware, 5-1/4 in. high. *Girard Foundation Collection. Museum of International Folk Art. Photograph by Michael Monteaux A.1982.20.51.*

# Peanut Butter Cheesecake with Peanut Brittle

2 (8-ounce) packages cream cheese, softened

1-1/4 cups creamy peanut butter (do not use old-fashioned style or freshly ground)

1 cup sugar

3/4 cup sour cream

3 large eggs

2 teaspoons vanilla

1 (11-ounce) package peanut butter chips

TOPPING

2 cups lightly toasted unsalted shelled peanuts

1 cup sugar

1 cup light corn syrup

1 tablespoon baking soda

1 tablespoon apricot jam, warmed

SERVES 12

Preheat oven to 325 degrees F. Spray a 9-inch diameter springform pan with nonstick vegetable oil spray. Line the bottom of the pan with parchment paper. Double-wrap the outside of the pan with heavy-duty aluminum foil.

Using an electric mixer, beat cream cheese, peanut butter, and sugar in a large bowl until well blended and fluffy. Beat in sour cream. Beat in eggs, 1 at a time, and then vanilla. Stir in peanut butter chips. Transfer batter to the prepared pan.

Place springform pan in a large roasting pan. Fill roasting pan with enough hot water to come 1 inch up the sides of the springform pan. Bake cake until it is slightly firm to the touch and the top appears dry, about 1 hour. Refrigerate cake uncovered until cold, at least 4 hours. Can be prepared 2 days ahead; cover and keep refrigerated.

*For the topping*: (This recipe makes about 1-1/2 pounds of peanut brittle, of which 1-1/2 cups are used for topping the cheesecake.) Line a large baking sheet with parchment paper, and then butter the parchment. Stir peanuts, sugar, and corn syrup in a heavy large saucepan over medium heat until sugar dissolves. Increase heat to high and boil, stirring frequently, until a candy thermometer registers 295 degrees F, about 20 minutes. Remove from heat. Add baking soda and stir briskly to blend (mixture will foam up). Immediately pour onto the prepared baking sheet. Spread brittle in an even layer. Let stand until cold and hard.

Break brittle into pieces. Store in airtight containers at room temperature. Can be prepared one month ahead.

To serve cheesecake, cut around pan sides to loosen cheesecake; release sides. Invert cake onto platter; peel off parchment. Brush apricot jam over top of cake. Sprinkle 1-1/2 cups peanut brittle pieces over cake and serve.

# Lemon Cheesecake with Fresh Blueberry Compote

SERVES 10 TO 12

## CRUST

Butter

1/4 cup graham cracker crumbs

## FILLING

4 (8-ounce) packages cream cheese, at room temperature

1-3/4 cups sugar

3/4 cup whipping cream

1/4 cup fresh lemon juice

1 tablespoon grated lemon zest

2 teaspoons vanilla

6 large eggs

## COMPOTE

4 (1/2-pint) baskets fresh blueberries

2/3 cup sugar

2 tablespoons fresh lemon juice

2 tablespoons water

*For the crust*: Preheat oven to 350 degrees F. Generously butter bottom and sides of a 9-inch-diameter springform pan. Place graham cracker crumbs in pan; tilt pan to allow crumbs to coat inside of pan. Shake out extra crumbs. Wrap outside of pan with two layers of heavy-duty aluminum foil.

*For the filling*: Using an electric mixer, beat cream cheese and sugar in a large bowl until well blended. With mixer running, slowly add cream, lemon juice, zest, and vanilla. Add eggs, 2 at a time, beating until just blended after each addition. Pour mixture into prepared pan.

Place springform pan in a large roasting pan. Pour enough warm water into roasting pan to come halfway up the sides of springform pan. Bake cheesecake until puffed, golden, and beginning to crack at the edges, about 75 minutes. Remove cheesecake from water. Refrigerate cheesecake uncovered until cold, about 4 hours. Cheesecake can be prepared up to 2 days ahead. Cover and refrigerate.

*For the compote*: Combine all ingredients in a heavy large skillet. Cook over medium heat until sugar dissolves and juices form, stirring occasionally. Bring to a boil. Mash some berries with the back of a fork and cook until mixture thickens slightly, about 6 minutes. Cool completely, then refrigerate until cold, about 1 hour. Can be made 1 day ahead. Cover and keep refrigerated.

Run a knife around the sides of the cheesecake; release springform pan sides. Transfer cheesecake to a serving plate. Serve, passing the blueberry compote separately.

# House of Luddingston Cheesecake

3 (8-ounce) packages cream cheese, at room temperature

4 egg whites

1 cup sugar

1 teaspoon vanilla

2/3 cup zwieback crumbs (or biscotti crumbs)

TOPPING

2 cups sour cream

2 tablespoons sugar

1 teaspoon vanilla

Shaved almonds, toasted

Fresh fruit for garnish

SERVES 12

Cream the cheese well to soften. Beat egg whites until stiff, then gradually add sugar. Blend egg whites and cream cheese together. Add vanilla and blend. Butter the sides and bottom of a 9-inch springform pan. Sprinkle zwieback crumbs on bottom of pan. Gently pour the cheese mixture into pan. Bake at 350 degrees F for 25 minutes.

*For the topping*: While cheesecake bakes, prepare the topping by blending sour cream, sugar, and vanilla together. After cheesecake is baked, spread topping over warm cheesecake. Sprinkle with toasted almonds. Bake 5 minutes more in a 475-degree F oven. Chill at least 2 hours. Garnish with fresh fruit.

## Quick Chocolate Cinnamon Mousse with Cherries

**CHERRIES**

8 ounces fresh Bing cherries, pitted

1/3 cup black cherry preserves

1/3 cup ruby port or cherry juice

**MOUSSE**

1-1/4 cups chilled heavy whipping cream, divided

1/8 teaspoon (generous) ground cinnamon

4 ounces bittersweet or semi-sweet chocolate, chopped

SERVES 4

*For the cherries*: Combine cherries, cherry preserves, and port in heavy small saucepan. Bring to a boil over high heat. Reduce heat to medium and boil until juices thicken to syrup consistency, stirring frequently, about 10 minutes. Remove from heat. Transfer to a small bowl and chill until cold, about 3 hours. Can be made 1 day ahead. Cover and keep chilled.

*For the mousse*: Combine 1/4 cup cream and cinnamon in a small saucepan; bring to a boil. Remove from heat. Add chocolate and whisk until melted and smooth. Transfer chocolate mixture to a large bowl. Using an electric mixer, beat remaining cream in a medium bowl until soft peaks form. Fold one-fourth of whipped cream into lukewarm chocolate mixture. Fold remaining whipped cream into chocolate mixture in 3 additions, just until incorporated. Divide mousse among 4 glasses or bowls. Chill until set, about 4 hours. Can be made 1 day ahead. Cover and keep chilled.

To serve, spoon cherries with syrup over mousse.

## Puff Pastry Summer Dessert Pizza

1/2 (17.3-ounce) package puff pastry

1 (12-ounce) jar lemon curd

Dessert wine, or late-harvest wine

Seasonal fruit or berries

Bert Geer Phillips (1868–1956), *Our Washerwoman's Family—New Mexico*, c. 1918. Oil on canvas, 40-1/2 x 41-5/8 in. Collection of New Mexico Museum of Art. Gift of Governor and Mrs. Arthur Seligman, before 1930. Photograph by Blair Clark.

SERVES 6

Roll out the puff pastry on a floured surface to make a rectangle. Place on a baking sheet and turn edges of pastry in to make a small "pie" edge. Prick pastry center several times with a fork. Bake according to package directions, or until golden brown. Cool to room temperature.

Meanwhile, whisk lemon curd with enough dessert wine to make a spread. Cover and save at room temperature until serving. Rinse and dry fruit or berries and store in the refrigerator.

Just before serving, spread lemon curd mixture over the pastry, and then arrange fruit or berries on top. Cut and serve.

# Kahlúa Amaretto Slush

1 quart coffee ice cream

1 pint French vanilla ice cream

1/2 cup Kahlúa (or coffee liqueur)

1/4 cup amaretto liqueur

6 amaretti cookies

SERVES 6

Soften ice creams and put in a large bowl; mix well. Mix in Kahlúa and amaretto; freeze. This can be made up to 3 to 4 weeks in advance.

Remove from freezer when guests arrive so the Kahlúa slush will be soupy by dessert time. Serve in champagne flutes with a wide-mouthed straw and accompany each serving with an amaretti cookie.

# Versatile Ice Cream Bombe

3 or 4 different flavored ice creams

Chopped nuts or cookie crumbs

SERVES 4

Soften the lightest color of flavored ice creams. Pour into the base of an upright 1-quart glass mixing bowl, filling to 1/4 to 1/3 of the bowl. Freeze. When the first layer is frozen, soften the second flavored ice cream and pour on top of the first layer. Freeze. Repeat layers till bowl is almost filled. (Jams or fruits can be added to the top of a frozen layer before pouring in the next layer. Chocolate syrup does not work well between layers.)

After freezing the last and darkest layer of the flavored ice creams, top with a thin layer of chopped nuts or cookie crumbs to make the base for the bombe when it is inverted. Cover and freeze. Can be made 1 to 2 weeks before serving.

To serve, remove from the freezer, dip frozen bombe in a bowl of warm water to loosen edges. Invert onto a serving plate and place back in the freezer for 5 to 10 minutes. Cut into serving-size pieces.

*Voilá, the versatile bombe.*

# Caramelized Apples with Dried Cranberries over Ice Cream

2 tablespoons unsalted butter

2 apples (3/4 pound) peeled, cored, and cut into 1/4-inch-wide wedges

1/4 cup dried cranberries or tart cherries

2/3 cup sugar

1/8 teaspoon salt

1-1/2 teaspoons fresh lemon juice, divided

1/2 cup heavy cream

Vanilla ice cream or frozen yogurt

SERVES 4

Heat butter in a 12-inch heavy skillet over moderately high heat until foam subsides. Sauté apples and dried cranberries, stirring and turning over occasionally, until apples are just beginning to brown, about 2 to 3 minutes. Add sugar, salt, and 1/2 teaspoon lemon juice. Increase heat to high and cook, stirring, until juices are deep golden, about 5 minutes. Add cream and boil, stirring, 1 minute. Remove from heat and cool to warm, about 15 minutes. Stir in remaining 1 teaspoon lemon juice. Serve warm over ice cream.

Edward Kemp, *Cowgirl at San Gabriel Ranch, Alcalde, NM*, c. 1910–1920. Collection of the Palace of the Governors Photo Archives.

## Chocolate Pecan "Tout de Sweet"

1 box Duncan Hines chocolate cake mix

1 cup unsalted butter, melted

1 cup chopped toasted pecans

MAKES 24 TO 30

Preheat oven to 350 degrees F. Combine cake mix and melted butter in a large bowl and mix until smooth; mix in pecans. Drop teaspoons of mixture on an ungreased baking sheet about 2 inches apart. Bake 12 minutes, or until firm. Cool before removing from sheet.

## Almond "Tout de Sweet"

1 box Duncan Hines yellow cake mix

1 cup unsalted butter, melted

1 teaspoon vanilla

1 cup sliced almonds, toasted

MAKES 24 TO 30

Preheat oven to 350 degrees F. Combine cake mix, butter, and vanilla in a large bowl and mix until smooth; mix in almonds. Drop teaspoons of mixture on an ungreased baking sheet about 2 inches apart. Bake 12 minutes, or until light brown. Loosen cookies with a spatula while warm. Remove from the baking sheet and cool.

# Chocolate Croissant Bread Pudding

6 fresh croissants

2 pounds Ghirardelli semisweet chocolate

1/4 cup butter, at room temperature

8 eggs

3 cups heavy cream

1 cup sugar

1 cup Godiva liqueur

Confectioners' sugar

SERVES 8 TO 10

Place croissants in a 8 x 12-inch buttered baking dish. Melt chocolate and butter in a double boiler; remove from heat. In a large bowl, mix eggs, cream, sugar, liqueur, and chocolate mixture together until smooth. Pour mixture over croissants and let soak 1 to 2 hours.

Bake 20 to 25 minutes in a 325-degree F oven. Dust with confectioners' sugar and serve warm.

# Chocolate Lime Sauce with Summer Fruit

2 cups heavy cream

12 ounces white chocolate, broken into 1/2-inch pieces

2 teaspoons lime zest

4 cups assorted fruit

2 cups berries

Fresh mint

SERVES 10 TO 12

Heat cream in a double boiler until the edges begin to bubble. Remove from heat; add chocolate pieces and blend until smooth. Add zest. Sauce can be made ahead and kept in the refrigerator. Rewarm before serving.

Mix assorted fruit and berries in a large bowl. Transfer to individual serving dishes and pour chocolate lime sauce over fruit.

Garnish with fresh mint.

# Chocolate Ganache

1 pound semisweet or bittersweet chocolate, coarsely chopped

1 cup heavy cream

2 tablespoons sugar

2 tablespoons unsalted butter

1 to 2 tablespoons dark rum (or brandy, Kahlúa, or Grand Marnier)

1 teaspoon vanilla

MAKES 2 CUPS

Place chocolate in a large bowl. Combine the cream, sugar, and butter in a small saucepan. Place over medium heat and stir constantly until the butter melts. Heat until bubbles start to form around the edges of the pan and the cream is just about to boil.

Immediately pour the hot cream over the chocolate. Let the mixture sit for 30 seconds to soften the chocolate. Stir gently until smooth and thick. Stir in the rum and vanilla.

While the ganache is warm and liquid, use as a dessert sauce or as a glaze for tarts. Or chill the ganache for 30 minutes, or until firm.

Chilled ganache can be formed into bite-size truffles or used as a filling to sandwich macaroons, meringues, or other cookies.

To return chilled ganache to its liquid state, reheat in a double boiler over barely simmering water, stirring occasionally until melted. Ganache can be refrigerated for up to 1 week.

# Simple Chocolate Sauce

6 ounces Scharffen Berger 70%
bittersweet chocolate, broken
into pieces

1/4 cup low-fat milk or water

2 tablespoons sugar

MAKES 1/2 CUP

Place broken chocolate and milk in a small heavy saucepan over low heat, stirring constantly. As the chocolate begins to melt, add sugar. Continue to stir slowly until all ingredients are incorporated. Additional liquid can be added as needed.

Pour over ice cream, pound cake, or fruit.

Sauce can be kept stored in the refrigerator for about 2 weeks and reheated as needed.

# Champagne Syrup over Raspberries

1 (750-ml) bottle champagne or
other sparkling wine, divided

2 tablespoons unflavored gelatin

3/4 cup sugar

1 1/2 pint fresh raspberries

SERVES 6 TO 8

Pour 1/2 cup champagne into a small bowl and sprinkle the gelatin over it. Let sit undisturbed for about 5 minutes. Meanwhile, pour the remaining champagne into a medium saucepan and add the sugar. Warm over medium heat, stirring occasionally, until the sugar dissolves. Simmer until the liquid reduces to about 2-1/2 cups. Remove from the heat and whisk in the gelatin-champagne mixture until dissolved.

Place the raspberries in 6 to 8 wine glasses, preferably, or into dessert bowls. With a liquid measuring cup, or small ladle, dip out the champagne syrup and pour it equally over the berries. Refrigerate for at least 2 hours, and up to a day, if you wish. The syrup should be somewhat jellied and lightly set, not firm. Serve cold.

*All quivery and see-through, sparkling syrup and fresh raspberries make this light dessert perfect for a garden lunch or dinner on a summer evening on the patio.*

—*Cheryl Alters Jamison, cookbook author from Santa Fe*

Anonymous artist, *Mescal Jar*, c. 1935. San Bartolo Coyotepec, Oaxaca, Mexico. Painted earthenware, 20 in. high. Girard Foundation Collection. Museum of International Folk Art. Photograph by Michael Monteaux. AGEx23.5.

# Crème Anglaise with Brown-Sugared Strawberries

STRAWBERRIES

3 cups halved strawberries

1/3 cup firmly packed brown sugar

CRÈME ANGLAISE

1/4 cup sugar

1/4 teaspoon salt

2 large eggs

2 cups milk

1 teaspoon vanilla extract

1/8 teaspoon almond extract

Fresh mint sprigs for garnish

SERVES 4

*For the strawberries:* Combine strawberries and sugar; let stand at room temperature for 30 minutes.

*For the crème anglaise:* Combine sugar, salt, and eggs in a large bowl, stirring well with a whisk. Heat milk in a small heavy saucepan over medium-high heat to 180 degrees F, or until tiny bubbles form around the edge (do not boil). Gradually add milk to egg mixture, stirring constantly with a whisk. Return milk mixture to the pan; cook over medium-low heat 5 minutes, or until slightly thick and mixture coats the back of a spoon, stirring constantly. Remove from heat, stir in vanilla and almond extracts.

Serve warm or chilled over strawberries. Garnish with fresh mint sprigs, if desired.

*The crème anglaise custard will be pourable when done and will thicken only slightly when chilled.*

# Warm Berry Compote

1/4 cup water

1/2 cup sugar

2 cups quartered strawberries

1 cup blueberries

1 cup blackberries

2 teaspoons fresh lemon juice

Pinch of salt

1/4 cup unsalted butter, at room temperature, cut into 1/4-inch cubes

Vanilla ice cream

SERVES 4

In a large, nonreactive sauté pan over medium heat, combine water and sugar and bring to a boil, stirring to dissolve the sugar. Cook for 2 minutes, then add the strawberries, blueberries, blackberries, lemon juice, and salt. Return to a boil, add the butter, and swirl the mixture in the pan until the butter melts.

Spoon berries and sauce onto warmed dessert plates, and place a small scoop of vanilla ice cream in the center of each plate. Serve immediately.


# Rich Chocolate Sauce

1 cup sugar

1 cup boiling water

4 ounces bittersweet chocolate

2 teaspoons cornstarch

1/2 cup whipping cream

Pinch of salt

1 tablespoon butter

MAKES 1/2 CUP

Combine sugar with boiling water. Add chocolate and stir until it melts. Stir in cornstarch and mix well. Add whipping cream and stir on low heat until thickened. Add a pinch of salt, if desired. Add butter, combining well. Serve warm.

*The taste of the sauce depends on the quality of the chocolate used. The sauce can be kept refrigerated or frozen. Warm slowly in the microwave and serve over ice cream.*


# Alice B. Toklas Figs over Ice Cream

2 pounds dried figs

2 (3-inch) cinnamon sticks

12 whole cloves

1 cup firmly packed dark brown sugar

1 cup firmly packed light brown sugar

1/2 teaspoon grated lemon zest

1/4 teaspoon grated orange zest

4 cups ruby port

1 cup dry red wine

Vanilla ice cream

SERVES 12

In a saucepan combine figs, cinnamon sticks, cloves, sugars, zests, port, and red wine. Simmer covered for 1 hour, or until figs are tender. Let stand in a cool place for 24 hours. Then chill until you are ready to use.

May be made ahead 5 to 7 days and stored in the refrigerator.

When ready to serve, remove cloves and cinnamon sticks. Serve over vanilla ice cream.

# Brandied Berries and Ice Cream

I quart raspberries

I quart blueberries

I quart peaches, peeled and
  quartered

2 quarts vanilla ice cream,
  softened

Peach brandy, to taste

SERVES 4 TO 6

Reserve some fresh berries for garnish. Mix fruit and ice cream with a wooden spoon until it reaches the consistency of a milkshake, adding the ice cream slowly so the fruit isn't bruised. Add peach brandy to ice cream. (You may choose not to use the full amount of ice cream.)

Divide among 4 to 6 parfait dishes or margarita glasses.

May be kept in freezer for 1 to 2 days. Remove and let sit for 5 to 10 minutes before serving.

# Sugared Walnuts

2 cups firmly packed brown sugar

I cup sugar

I cup sour cream

I teaspoon vanilla

9 cups walnuts

SERVES 10 TO 12

Bring sugars and sour cream to a rolling boil. Cook to soft-ball stage (240 degrees F). Stir in vanilla; add nuts. Once nuts are coated, spread on aluminum foil to cool. Break apart and store in airtight container. Use as a dessert topping over ice cream and yogurts.

# Pear Sauce

5 cups peeled and chopped ripe
  Bartlett pears

1/2 cup sugar

I lemon, peeled and sectioned

3/4 cup coarsely chopped walnuts

1/2 cup golden raisins

1/4 cup dried sweet cherries

I navel orange, peeled and
  sectioned

MAKES 4 CUPS

Combine pears and sugar in a ziplock plastic bag; shake well. Seal and refrigerate 8 hours or overnight.

Place 2 tablespoons lemon sections in a medium saucepan; reserve remaining lemon sections for another use. Add pear mixture, walnuts, raisins, cherries, and orange to pan. Bring to a simmer over medium heat. Cook 30 minutes, or until mixture is thick and slightly soft, stirring occasionally.

*Great over ice cream or pound cake.*

*The sauce can be made up to 2 days ahead and warmed in the microwave just before serving. You will get a lot of liquid from the pears after they macerate in the sugar overnight.*

# Apricot-Lavender Sauce

1 cup sugar

1/2 cup water

3 pounds fresh apricots, halved and pitted (about 8 cups)

1-1/2 teaspoons chopped fresh lavender (or 1/2 teaspoon dried)

MAKES 3 CUPS

Combine sugar, water, and apricots in a large, heavy saucepan. Cook over high heat 3 minutes, or until the sugar dissolves, stirring constantly. Reduce heat to medium; cook 30 minutes, or until fruit breaks down and mixture is slightly thick, stirring frequently.

Remove from heat. Stir in lavender, let stand 10 minutes. Strain through a sieve into a large bowl; discard solids. Cool to room temperature. Cover and chill. This sauce will store refrigerated for 2 weeks.

*Great over ice cream, fresh ricotta cheese, yogurt, or angel food cake.*

*The sauce has a beautiful color and unforgettable flavor. It may be served cold, at room temperature, or slightly warm.*

# Caramel Rainbow Parfait

Any fresh fruit, such as peaches, nectarines, or berries

1 pint frozen fruit yogurt or sorbet

1 pint vanilla ice cream

Caramel sauce, purchased, warmed

1/4 cup chopped pecans, toasted

SERVES 4

Place a bit of sliced fresh fruit or berries in the bottom of 4 clear serving glasses or bowls. Add a layer of frozen yogurt, followed by another layer of fruit, ending with a layer of vanilla ice cream.

Drizzle warm caramel sauce over and sprinkle with chopped pecans.

# Tequila Sorbet

1 pint lemon sorbet

1/4 cup good-quality tequila

Zest of 2 limes, finely grated

SERVES 4

Using an ice cream scoop, spoon 2 scoops of sorbet into each of 4 glasses.

Drizzle 1 tablespoon tequila over sorbet in each glass and sprinkle with lime zest.

Serve immediately.

## Metric Conversion Chart

Liquid and Dry Measures

| U.S. | Canadian | Australian |
|---|---|---|
| 1/4 teaspoon | 1 mL | 1 ml |
| 1/2 teaspoon | 2 mL | 2 ml |
| 1 teaspoon | 5 mL | 5 ml |
| 1 tablespoon | 15 mL | 20 ml |
| 1/4 cup | 50 mL | 60 ml |
| 1/3 cup | 75 mL | 80 ml |
| 1/2 cup | 125 mL | 125 ml |
| 2/3 cup | 150 mL | 170 ml |
| 3/4 cup | 175 mL | 190 ml |
| 1 cup | 250 mL | 250 ml |
| 1 quart | 1 liter | 1 litre |

## Temperature Conversion Chart

| Fahrenheit | Celsius |
|---|---|
| 250 | 120 |
| 275 | 140 |
| 300 | 150 |
| 325 | 160 |
| 350 | 180 |
| 375 | 190 |
| 400 | 200 |
| 425 | 220 |
| 450 | 230 |
| 475 | 240 |
| 500 | 260 |

# Dessert Cookbook Committee and Contributors

*Dessert Cookbook Co-chairs*
Liz Crews
Mary Anne Larsen

*Dessert Cookbook Committee*
Joan Dayton
Terry Greenfield
Valerie Hamilton
Maryann McCaffery
John O'Malley
Doris Roland
Yvonne Russell
Enid Tidwell
Ann Wallace

*Cookbook Project Chairman*
Dorothy Black

*Cookbook Project Advisor*
John Stafford

*Contributors*
Jane Adams
Charmay Allred
Earlene Allred
Andy Barnes, Chef, Dinner For Two
Sharon C. Bennett
Dorothy Bracey
Jane Buchsbaum
Mary Costello-Campbell
Gloria Cowen
Sandra Crawford
Liz Crews
Hector Cruz
Susan Curtis, The Santa Fe School of Cooking
Joan Dayton
Leslie DeVera-Duncan
Rosalind Doherty
Colleen Duncan
Viki Tilford Edwards
Angel Estrada, Executive Chef, Santacafé
Madelyn Farris
Joan Gibbons
Joan Gillcrist, Andiamo Restaurant
Terry Greenfield
Gabrielle Hakki
Dottie Hammel
Anne W. Hodde
Harriet Holleman

Patsy Hutchison
Paula Hutchison
John Ireland
Cheryl Alters Jamison, Santa Fe cookbook author
Carolyn Jenkins
Robert Johnson
Mary Anne Larsen
Linda Laughlin
Lindsley Lee
Louise Leopold
Wanda McQueen
Gena McKee
Carolyn Minton
Bobby Morean
Linda Morsman
Rosalea Murphy, The Pink Adobe Restaurant
Judith Newton
Donna Nordin, Executive Chef, Terra Cotta Restaurant
Beatriz Ordoñez
Bernadette Pesenti-Valdes
Ann Price
Helen West Pynn
Doris Roland
Dee Rusanowski, Le Saveur Restaurant
Yvonne Russell
Joan B. Scheinberg
Joan Schoenberg
Marian Silver
Gail Sirna
John Stafford
Carole Stepp
Janet Stickel
Jeannette Strawbridge
Emily Swanter, Santa Fe Cooking instructor
Enid Tidwell
Susan Thompson
Benedicte Valentiner
Virginia G. Vigil, Executive Chef, Isaac's Table, Ellis Store Country Inn
John Vollertsen, Director, Las Cosas Cooking School
Margie Smith Voss
Nancy Waldman
Ann Wallace
Gail Willson
Anne Wooldridge

# Index